Holt McDougal Mathematics

Course 2
Homework and Practice Workbook

HOLT McDOUGAL
a division of Houghton Mifflin Harcourt

Printed in the United States of America

ISBN 13: 978-0-55-401402-9
ISBN 10: 0-55-401402-5

7 8 9 1421 13 12 11
4500307796

Contents

LESSON 1-1

Practice B

Numbers and Patterns

Identify a possible pattern. Use the pattern to write the next three numbers.

1. 41, 37, 33, 29, ____, ____, ____, ...

____

____

2. 50, 52, 56, 62, ____, ____, ____, ...

____

____

3. 320, 160, 80, 40, ____, ____, ____, ...

____

____

4. 24, 40, 56, 72, ____, ____, ____, ...

____

____

Identify a possible pattern. Use the pattern to draw the next three figures.

5. 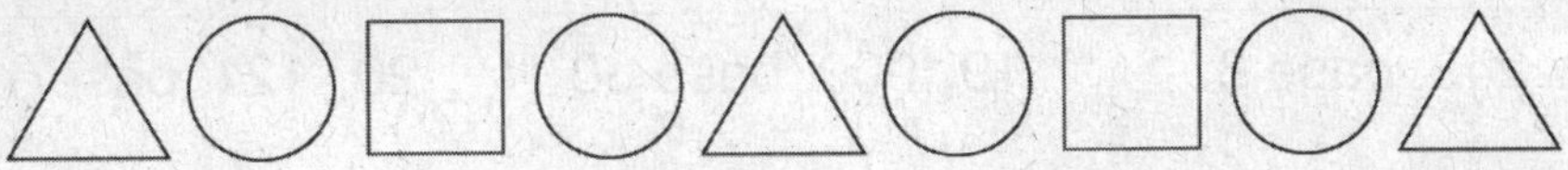

____

6. 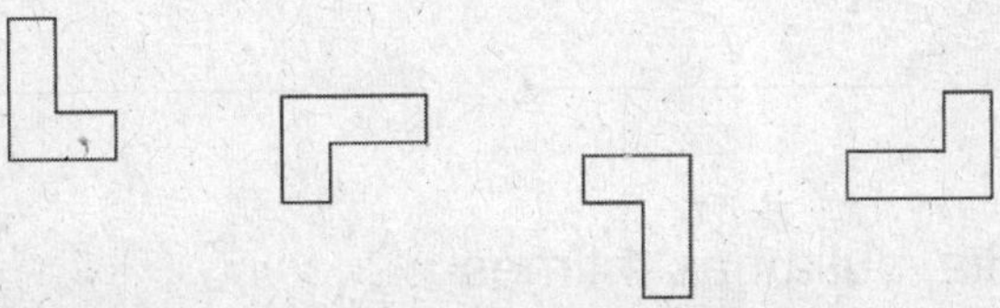

____

7. Complete the table so that it shows the number of dots in each figure.

Figure 1 **Figure 2** **Figure 3** **Figure 4** **Figure 5**

Figure	1	2	3
Number of Dots			

How many dots are in the fifth figure of the pattern? ____

Use drawings to justify your answer.

Name ________________ Date ________________ Class ________________

LESSON 1-2

Practice B

Exponents

Find each value.

1. 5^2 ________
2. 2^4 ________
3. 3^3 ________
4. 7^2 ________
5. 4^4 ________
6. 12^2 ________
7. 10^3 ________
8. 11^1 ________
9. 1^6 ________
10. 20^2 ________
11. 6^3 ________
12. 7^3 ________

Write each number using an exponent and the given base.

13. 16, base 4 ________
14. 25, base 25 ________
15. 100, base 10 ________
16. 125, base 5 ________
17. 32, base 2 ________
18. 243, base 3 ________
19. 900, base 30 ________
20. 121, base 11 ________
21. 3,600, base 60 ________
22. 256, base 4 ________
23. 512, base 8 ________
24. 196, base 14 ________

25. Damon has 4 times as many stamps as Julia. Julia has 4 times as many stamps as Claire. Claire has 4 stamps. Write the number of stamps Damon has in both exponential form and standard form.

____

26. Holly starts a jump rope exercise program. She jumps rope for 3 minutes the first week. In the second week, she triples the time she jumps. In the third week, she triples the time of the second week, and in the fourth week, she triples the time of the third week. How many minutes does she jump rope during the fourth week?

____

Name ______________________ Date ______________ Class ______________

LESSON 1-3

Practice B

Scientific Notation

Multiply.

1. $6 \cdot 10^3$ ______
2. $22 \cdot 10^1$ ______
3. $8 \cdot 10^2$ ______
4. $18 \cdot 10^0$ ______
5. $70 \cdot 10^2$ ______
6. $25 \cdot 10^3$ ______
7. $3 \cdot 10^4$ ______
8. $180 \cdot 10^3$ ______
9. $84 \cdot 10^4$ ______
10. $315 \cdot 10^2$ ______
11. $210 \cdot 10^3$ ______
12. $1{,}004 \cdot 10^3$ ______
13. $1{,}764 \cdot 10^1$ ______
14. $856 \cdot 10^0$ ______
15. $4{,}055 \cdot 10^3$ ______
16. $716 \cdot 10^4$ ______

Write each number in scientific notation.

17. 34,000 ______
18. 7,700 ______
19. 2,100,000 ______
20. 404,000 ______
21. 21,000,000 ______
22. 612.00 ______
23. 3,001,000 ______
24. $62.13 \cdot 10^4$ ______

25. Lake Superior covers an area of about 31,700 square miles. Write this number in scientific notation.

____

26. Mars is about $1.42 \cdot 10^8$ miles from the sun. Write this number in standard form.

____

27. In 2005, the population of China was about $1.306 \cdot 10^9$. What was the population of China written in standard form?

____

28. A scientist estimates there are 4,800,000 bacteria in a test tube. How does she record the number using scientific notation?

____

Name ______________________ Date ______________ Class ______________

LESSON 1-4

Practice B

Order of Operations

Simplify each expression.

1. $15 \cdot 3 + 12 \cdot 2$

2. $212 + 21 \div 3$

3. $9 \cdot 3 - 18 \div 3$

4. $65 - 36 \div 3$

5. $100 - 9^2 + 2$

6. $3 \cdot 5 - 45 \div 3^2$

7. $54 \div 6 + 4 \cdot 6$

8. $(6 + 5) \cdot 16 \div 2$

9. $60 - 8 \cdot 12 \div 3$

10. $45 - 3^2 \cdot 5$

11. $52 - (8 \cdot 2 \div 4) + 3^2$

12. $(2^3 + 10 \div 2) \cdot 3$

13. $25 + 7(18 - 4^2)$

14. $(6 \cdot 3 - 12)^2 \div 9 + 7$

15. $4^3 - (3 + 12 \cdot 2 - 9)$

16. $2^4 \div 8 + 5$

17. $(1 + 2)^2 \cdot (3 - 1)^2 \div 2$

18. $(16 \div 4) + 4 \cdot (2^2 - 2)$

19. $2^5 - (3 \cdot 7 - 7)$

20. $75 + 5^2 - (8 - 3)$

21. $9 \cdot 6 - 5(10 - 3)$

22. $96 \div 4 + 5 \cdot 2^2$

23. $(15 - 6)^2 \div 3 - 3^3$

24. $19 - 8 \cdot 5 \div 10 + 6 \div 3$

25. Jared has $32. He buys 5 packs of trading cards that cost $3 each and a display book that costs $7. Simplify the expression $32 - (5 \cdot 3 + 7)$ to find out how much money Jared has left.

26. David buys 3 movie tickets for $6 each and 2 bags of popcorn for $2 each. Simplify the expression $3 \cdot 6 + 2 \cdot 2$ to find out how much money David spent in all.

Name ______________________ Date ____________ Class ____________

LESSON 1-5

Practice B

Properties of Numbers

Tell which property is represented.

1. 12 • 14 = 14 • 12

   ____

2. 1 • 36 = 36

   ____

3. (17 + 36) + 4 = 17 + (36 + 4)

   ____

4. 8 • 12 • 5 = 8 • (12 • 5)

   ____

Simplify each expression. Justify each step.

5. 4 • 9 • 50

   4 • 9 • 50 = ______________________

   = ______________________

   = ______________________

   = ______________________

6. (33 + 45) + 7

   (33 + 45) + 7 = ______________________

   = ______________________

   = ______________________

   = ______________________

Use the Distributive Property to find each product.

7. 3(26) = ______________________

   = ______________________

   = ______________________

   = ______________________

8. (18)9 = ______________________

   = ______________________

   = ______________________

   = ______________________

Name ______________________ Date ______________ Class ______________

LESSON 1-6

Practice B

Variables and Algebraic Expressions

Evaluate $n - 5$ for each value of n.

1. $n = 8$ ______
2. $n = 121$ ______
3. $n = 32$ ______
4. $n = 59$ ______

Evaluate each expression for the given values of the variable.

5. $3n + 15$ for $n = 4$ ______
6. $h \div 12$ for $h = 60$ ______
7. $32x - 32$ for $x = 2$ ______
8. $\frac{c}{2}$ for $c = 24$ ______
9. $(n \div 2)5$ for $n = 14$ ______
10. $8p + 148$ for $p = 15$ ______
11. $e^2 - 7$ for $e = 8$ ______
12. $3d^2 + d$ for $d = 5$ ______
13. $40 - 4k^3$ for $k = 2$ ______
14. $2y - z$ for $y = 21$ and $z = 19$ ______
15. $3h^2 + 8m$ for $h = 3$ and $m = 2$ ______
16. $18 \div a + b \div 9$ for $a = 6$ and $b = 45$ ______
17. $10x - 4y$ for $x = 14$ and $y = 5$ ______

18. You can find the area of a rectangle with the expression lw where l represents the length and w represents the width. What is the area of the rectangle at right in square feet?

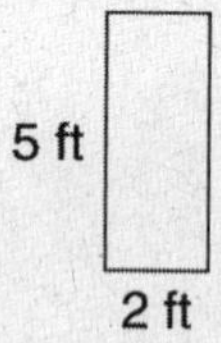

______

19. Rita drove an average of 55 mi/h on her trip to the mountains. You can use the expression $55h$ to find out how many miles she drove in h hours. If she drove for 5 hours, how many miles did she drive?

______

Name ________________________ Date ______________ Class ______________

LESSON 1-7

Practice B

Translating Words Into Math

Write each phrase as an algebraic expression.

1. 125 decreased by a number

____

2. 359 more than *z*

____

3. the product of a number and 35

____

4. the quotient of 100 and *w*

____

5. twice a number, plus 27

____

6. 12 less than 15 times *x*

____

7. the product of *e* and 4, divided by 12

____

8. *y* less than 18 times 6

____

9. 48 more than the quotient of a number and 64 ______________________

10. 500 less than the product of 4 and a number ______________________

11. the quotient of *p* and 4, decreased by 320 ______________________

12. 13 multiplied by the amount 60 minus *w* ______________________

13. the quotient of 45 and the sum of *c* and 17 ______________________

14. twice the sum of a number and 600 ______________________

15. There are twice as many flute players as there are trumpet players in the band. If there are *n* flute players, write an algebraic expression to find out how many trumpet players there are. ______________________

16. The Nile River is the longest river in the world at 4,160 miles. A group of explorers traveled along the entire Nile in *x* days. They traveled the same distance each day. Write an algebraic expression to find each day's distance. ______________________

17. A slice of pizza has 290 calories, and a stalk of celery has 5 calories. Write an algebraic expression to find out how many calories there are in *a* slices of pizza and *b* stalks of celery. ______________________

18. Grant pays 10¢ per minute plus $5 per month for telephone long distance. Write an algebraic expression for *m* minutes of long-distance calls in one month. ______________________

Name ______________________ Date ______________ Class ______________

LESSON 1-8

Practice B

Simplifying Algebraic Expressions

Identify like terms in each list.

1. $3a \quad b^2 \quad b^3 \quad 4b^2 \quad 4 \quad 5a$

____

2. $x \quad x^4 \quad 4x \quad 4x^2 \quad 4x^4 \quad 3x^2$

____

3. $6m \quad 6m^2 \quad n^2 \quad 2n \quad 2 \quad 4m \quad 5n$

____

4. $12s \quad 7s^4 \quad 9s \quad s^2 \quad 5 \quad 5s^4 \quad 2$

____

Simplify. Justify your steps using the Commutative, Associative, and Distributive Properties when necessary.

5. $2p + 22q^2 - p$

____

6. $x^2 + 3x^2 - 4^2$

____

7. $n^4 + n^3 + 3n - n - n^3$

____

8. $4a + 4b + 2 - 2a + 5b - 1$

____

9. $32m^2 + 14n^2 - 12m^2 + 5n - 3$

____

10. $2h^2 + 3g - 2h^2 + 2^2 - 3 + 4g$

____

11. Write an expression for the perimeter of the figure at the right. Then simplify the expression.

____

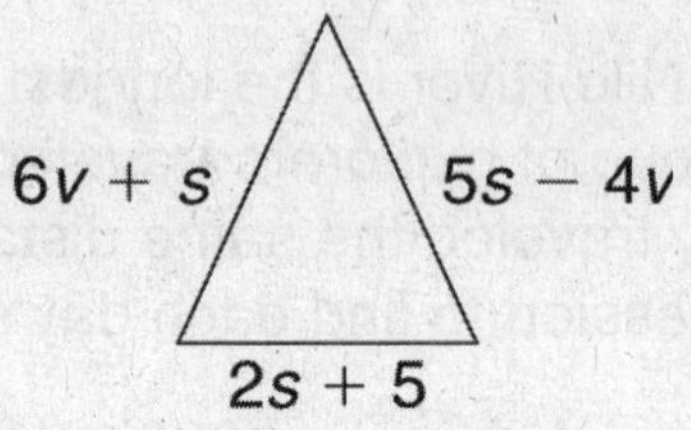

12. Write an expression for the combined perimeters of the figures at the right. Then simplify the expression.

____

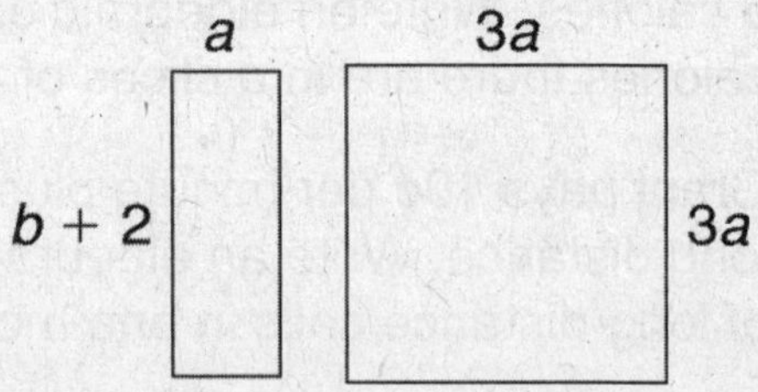

Name ______________________ Date ______________ Class ______________

LESSON 1-9

Practice B

Equations and Their Solutions

Determine whether the given value of the variable is a solution.

1. $a = 4$ for $12 - a = 6$
2. $m = 37$ for $23 + m = 60$
3. $x = 6$ for $54 = 9x$
4. $g = 96$ for $\frac{g}{4} = 32$
5. $n = 28$ for $n + 44 = 72$
6. $j = 6$ for $84 \div j = 12$
7. $k = 24$ for $3k = 6$
8. $m = 3$ for $42 = m + 39$
9. $y = 8$ for $8y + 6 = 70$
10. $s = 5$ for $18 = 3s - 3$
11. $k = 7$ for $23 - k = 30$
12. $v = 12$ for $84 = 7v$
13. $c = 15$ for $45 - 2c = 15$
14. $x = 10$ for $x + 25 - 2x + 4 = 19$
15. $e = 6$ for $42 = 51 - e$
16. $p = 15$ for $19 = p - 4$
17. Jason and Maya have their own web sites on the Internet. As of last week, Jason's web site had 2,426 visitors. This is twice as many visitors as Maya had. Did Maya have 1,213 visitors or 4,852 visitors to her web site?

    ____

18. Which problem situation best matches the equation $3c - 5 = 31$?

    Situation A: Rachel had a coupon for $5 off the cost of her order. She ordered 3 large pizzas that each cost the same amount and paid a total of $31. What was the cost of each pizza?

    Situation B: Rachel had a coupon for $31 off the cost of her order. She ordered 5 large pizzas that each cost the same amount and paid a total of $3. What was the cost of each pizza?

    ____

Name ______________________ Date ______________ Class ______________

LESSON 1-10

Practice B

Solving Equations by Adding or Subtracting

Solve each equation. Check your answer.

1. $33 = y - 44$ ________
2. $r - 32 = 77$ ________
3. $125 = x - 29$ ________
4. $k + 18 = 25$ ________
5. $589 + x = 700$ ________
6. $96 = 56 + t$ ________
7. $a - 9 = 57$ ________
8. $b - 49 = 254$ ________
9. $987 = f - 11$ ________
10. $32 + d = 1{,}400$ ________
11. $w - 24 = 90$ ________
12. $95 = g - 340$ ________
13. $e - 35 = 59$ ________
14. $84 = v + 30$ ________
15. $h + 15 = 81$ ________
16. $110 = a + 25$ ________
17. $45 + c = 91$ ________
18. $p - 29 = 78$ ________
19. $56 - r = 8$ ________
20. $39 = z + 8$ ________
21. $93 + g = 117$ ________

22. The Morales family is driving from Philadelphia to Boston. So far, they have driven 167 miles. This is 129 miles less than the total distance they must travel. How many miles is Philadelphia from Boston?

____

23. Ron has $1,230 in his savings account. This is $400 more than he needs to buy a new big screen TV. Write and solve an equation to find out how much the TV costs.

____

Name ______________________ Date ______________ Class ______________

LESSON 1-11

Practice B

Solving Equations by Multiplying or Dividing

Solve each equation. Check your answer.

1. $68 = \frac{r}{4}$ ______

2. $k \div 24 = 85$ ______

3. $255 = \frac{x}{4}$ ______

4. $42 = w \div 18$ ______

5. $\frac{a}{15} = 22$ ______

6. $82 = b \div 5$ ______

7. $\frac{c}{7} = 9$ ______

8. $28 = z \div 3$ ______

9. $\frac{y}{12} = 10$ ______

Solve each equation. Check your answer.

10. $52w = 364$ ______

11. $41x = 492$ ______

12. $410 = 82p$ ______

13. $35d = 735$ ______

14. $195 = 65h$ ______

15. $4k = 140$ ______

16. $110 = 5e$ ______

17. $27a = 216$ ______

18. $96 = 12n$ ______

19. Ashley earns $5.50 per hour babysitting. She wants to buy a CD player that costs $71.50, including tax. How many hours will she need to work to earn the money for the CD player?

______

20. A cat can jump the height of up to 5 times the length of its tail. How high can a cat jump if its tail is 13 inches long?

______

Name ______________________ Date ______________ Class ______________

LESSON 2-1

Practice B
Integers

Graph each integer and its opposite on a number line.

1. 8

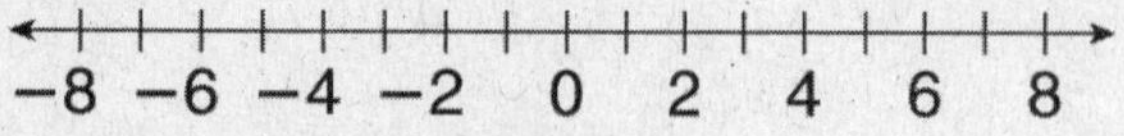

2. −7

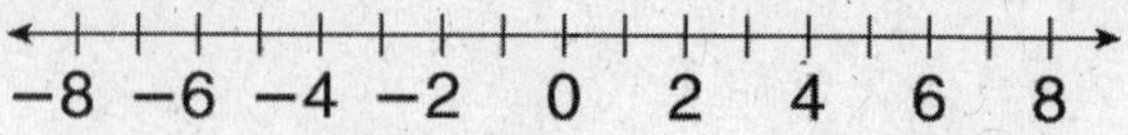

Compare the integers. Use < or >.

3. −15 ___ −7 4. 8 ___ −8 5. −14 ___ 13 6. −18 ___ −20

Use a number line to order the integers from least to greatest.

7. −1; 4; −5; 7; −3

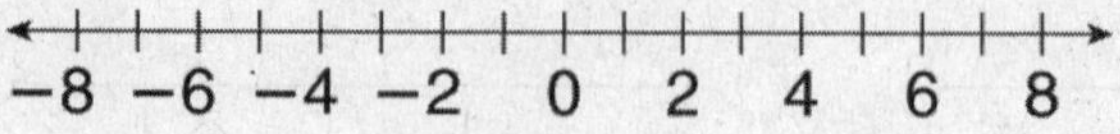

____

8. −6; 8; 0; 4; −2

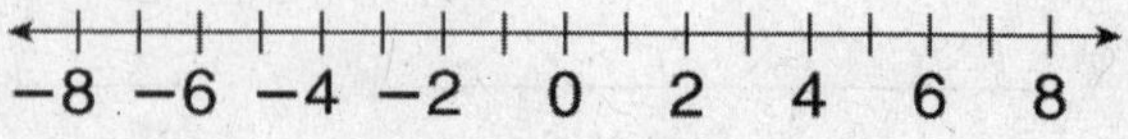

____

9. 6; 5; −7; −8; −2

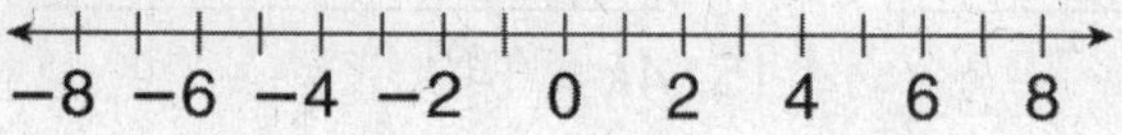

____

10. 1; 3; −4; −5; 7

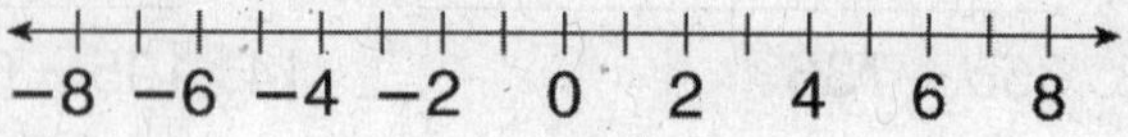

____

Use a number line to find each absolute value.

11. $|-18|$ ______ 12. $|11|$ ______ 13. $|-25|$ ______ 14. $|19|$ ______

15. $|-10|$ ______ 16. $|16|$ ______ 17. $|22|$ ______ 18. $|-14|$ ______

19. $|9|$ ______ 20. $|-24|$ ______ 21. $|-7|$ ______ 22. $|17|$ ______

23. Christy dove to a depth of 12 feet below the surface of the water. Write the depth as an integer.

____

24. The highest point in North Carolina is Mt. Mitchell, with a height of 6,684 feet. Write the height of Mt. Mitchell as an integer.

____

Name ______________________ Date ______________ Class ______________

LESSON 2-2

Practice B

Adding Integers

Use a number line to find each sum.

1. –1 + 5

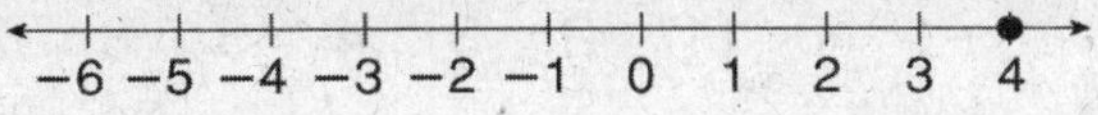

____

2. 4 + (–6)

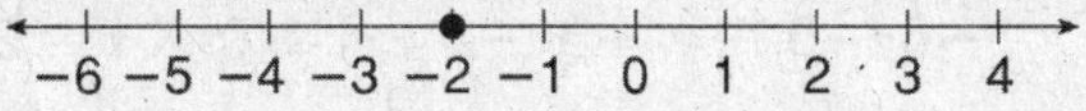

____

Find each sum.

3. –51 + (–9) ________

4. 27 + (–6) ________

5. 1 + (–30) ________

6. 15 + (–25) ________

7. 50 + (–7) ________

8. –19 + (–15) ________

9. (–23) + 9 ________

10. –19 + (–21) ________

11. –17 + 11 ________

12. 20 + (–8) ________

13. (–15) + (–7) ________

14. 12 + (–14) ________

Evaluate $e + f$ for the given values.

15. $e = 9$, $f = –24$ ________

16. $e = –17$, $f = –7$ ________

17. $e = 32$, $f = –19$ ________

18. $e = –15$, $f = –15$ ________

19. $e = –20$, $f = 20$ ________

20. $e = –30$, $f = 12$ ________

21. The temperature rose 9 °F in 3 hours. If the starting temperature was –5 °F, what was the final temperature?

____

22. Matt is playing a game. He gains 7 points, loses 10 points, gains 2 points, and then loses 8 points. What is his final score?

____

Name ______________________ Date ______________ Class ______________

LESSON 2-3

Practice B

Subtracting Integers

Use a number line to find each difference.

1. $-2 - 3$

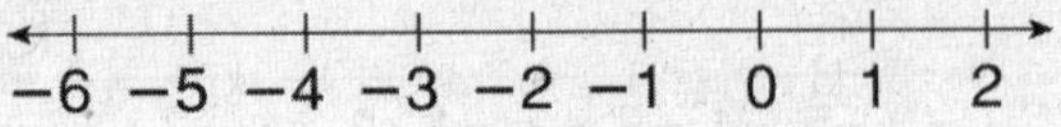

____

2. $5 - (-1)$

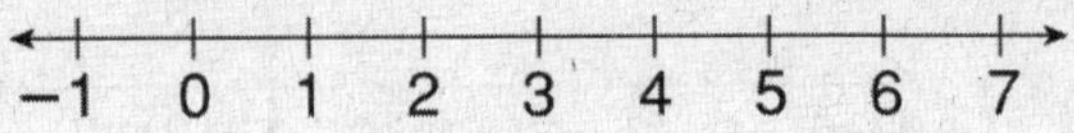

____

Find each difference.

3. $-6 - 4$ ______________

4. $-7 - (-12)$ ______________

5. $12 - 16$ ______________

6. $5 - (-19)$ ______________

7. $-18 - (-18)$ ______________

8. $23 - (-23)$ ______________

9. $-10 - (-9)$ ______________

10. $29 - (-13)$ ______________

11. $9 - 15$ ______________

12. $-12 - 14$ ______________

13. $22 - (-8)$ ______________

14. $-16 - (-11)$ ______________

Evaluate $x - y$ for each set of values.

15. $x = 14$, $y = -2$ ______________

16. $x = -11$, $y = 11$ ______________

17. $x = -8$, $y = -15$ ______________

18. $x = -9$, $y = -9$ ______________

19. $x = 9$, $y = -20$ ______________

20. $x = 20$, $y = 25$ ______________

21. The high temperature one day was –1 °F. The low temperature was –5 °F. What was the difference between the high and low temperatures for the day?

____

22. The temperature changed from 5 °F at 6 P.M. to –2 °F at midnight. How much did the temperature decrease?

____

Name ______________________ Date ______________ Class ______________

LESSON 2-4

Practice B

Multiplying and Dividing Integers

Find each product.

1. $8 \cdot (-5)$ ________
2. $-4 \cdot 7$ ________
3. $-6 \cdot (-3)$ ________
4. $-2 \cdot 4$ ________
5. $4 \cdot (-9)$ ________
6. $-9 \cdot 5$ ________
7. $6 \cdot 8$ ________
8. $-7 \cdot (-3)$ ________
9. $-6 \cdot (-6)$ ________
10. $9 \cdot (-3)$ ________
11. $-2 \cdot (-8)$ ________
12. $5 \cdot (-7)$ ________
13. $10 \cdot 8$ ________
14. $-5 \cdot 9$ ________
15. $9 \cdot (-6)$ ________
16. $(-4) \cdot (-11)$ ________

Find each quotient.

17. $25 \div (-5)$ ________
18. $-54 \div (-6)$ ________
19. $-10 \div 5$ ________
20. $-28 \div (-4)$ ________
21. $-42 \div (-7)$ ________
22. $-21 \div 0$ ________
23. $36 \div (-6)$ ________
24. $-81 \div (-9)$ ________
25. $-32 \div 8$ ________
26. $45 \div (-9)$ ________
27. $-72 \div (-8)$ ________
28. $50 \div 10$ ________
29. $-42 \div 6$ ________
30. $-72 \div (-9)$ ________
31. $40 \div 8$ ________
32. $56 \div 0$ ________

33. Kim was walking down a rocky path. For 4 minutes, the elevation dropped uniformly. Altogether it dropped 8 feet. What was the change in elevation per minute for the 4 minutes?

____

34. As a front passed, the temperature changed steadily over 6 hours. Altogether it changed −18 degrees. What was the change in temperature per hour for the 6 hours?

____

Name ____________________ Date ____________ Class ____________

LESSON 2-5

Practice B

Solving Equations Containing Integers

Solve each equation. Check your answer.

1. $n - 6 = -2$
2. $x - 8 = -11$
3. $7 = a - 5$
4. $y + 4 = 2$
5. $c + 7 = -3$
6. $0 = v + 1$
7. $8j = -16$
8. $-3k = 24$
9. $-20 = -4s$
10. $\frac{m}{-2} = -5$
11. $\frac{d}{6} = -3$
12. $\frac{r}{-7} = 4$
13. $p + 8 = -6$
14. $-15 = 5b$
15. $f - 9 = -1$
16. $\frac{n}{6} = -4$
17. $k + 10 = 3$
18. $4a = -16$
19. $-6x = -36$
20. $2 = e - 7$
21. $3 = \frac{m}{2}$
22. The temperature in Minnesota was –8 °F one day. This was 12 degrees less than the temperature in Indiana on the same day. What was the temperature in Indiana?

____

23. Mr. Harding sold 100 shares of stock at $14 per share. He had a loss of $6 per share. What did Mr. Harding pay for each share of the stock?

____

Name ______________________ Date ____________ Class ____________

LESSON 2-6

Practice B

Prime Factorization

Tell whether each number is prime or composite.

1. 33 ________
2. 41 ________
3. 52 ________
4. 79 ________
5. 96 ________
6. 121 ________
7. 83 ________
8. 119 ________

Write the prime factorization of each number.

9. 57 ________
10. 49 ________
11. 88 ________
12. 95 ________
13. 105 ________
14. 98 ________
15. 52 ________
16. 42 ________
17. 68 ________
18. 91 ________
19. 60 ________
20. 72 ________
21. 56 ________
22. 144 ________
23. 370 ________
24. 168 ________
25. 124 ________
26. 515 ________
27. 725 ________
28. 220 ________
29. 450 ________
30. 1,000 ________
31. 1,040 ________
32. 2,500 ________

33. The prime factorization of a number is $3^2 \cdot 5 \cdot 11$. What is the number?

____

Name ______________________ Date ______________ Class ______________

LESSON 2-7

Practice B

Greatest Common Factor

Find the greatest common factor (GCF).

1. 12, 15 ______________
2. 22, 33 ______________
3. 63, 45 ______________
4. 15, 50 ______________
5. 18, 81 ______________
6. 18, 48 ______________
7. 20, 24 ______________
8. 14, 42, 49 ______________
9. 3, 6, 9 ______________
10. 16, 24, 30 ______________
11. 16, 40, 88 ______________
12. 42, 70 ______________
13. 25, 125, 200 ______________
14. 26, 39, 52 ______________
15. 36, 100 ______________
16. 35, 77 ______________
17. 56, 84 ______________
18. 14, 49, 56, 84 ______________
19. 30, 75, 60, 90 ______________
20. 12, 38, 40, 94 ______________
21. 48, 66, 96, 102 ______________

22. Volunteers are preparing identical backpacks for refugees. There are 32 maps and 24 dictionaries to use for the backpacks. What is the greatest number of backpacks they can prepare using all of the maps and dictionaries?

____

23. Alyssa is preparing identical fruit baskets. There are 36 oranges and 60 apples to use for the baskets. What is the greatest number of fruit baskets she can prepare using all of the oranges and apples?

____

Name ______________________ Date ______________ Class ______________

LESSON 2-8

Practice B

Least Common Multiple

Find the least common multiple (LCM).

1. 8, 10 ________
2. 10, 15 ________
3. 6, 9 ________
4. 12, 16 ________
5. 18, 30 ________
6. 5, 11 ________
7. 15, 45 ________
8. 7, 28 ________
9. 4, 14 ________
10. 3, 10, 12 ________
11. 9, 36, 60 ________
12. 5, 15 ________
13. 7, 14, 49 ________
14. 8, 12, 24, 96 ________
15. 5, 25, 30 ________
16. 5, 9, 18 ________
17. 4, 10, 12, 15 ________
18. 4, 9, 12, 18 ________
19. 4, 12, 24, 36 ________
20. 24, 30, 48, 60 ________
21. 5, 9, 15, 18 ________

22. Jasmine is helping her father plant trees to create a border around the back yard. Jasmine plants a tree every 25 minutes, and her father plants a tree every 15 minutes. If they started together, how long before they would finish planting a tree at the same time?

____

23. Two dancers are rehearsing in a studio. One dancer's routine lasts 12 minutes. The other dancer's routine lasts 15 minutes. If they start together and take no breaks between their routines, how long before they start together again?

____

24. Evan and Renzo are swimming laps in the pool. It takes Evan 8 minutes to complete 1 lap and Renzo 6 minutes to complete 1 lap. They start together at the tops of their lanes. In how many minutes will they be together again at the tops of their lanes?

____

Name ______________________ Date ______________ Class ______________

LESSON 2-9

Practice B

Equivalent Fractions and Mixed Numbers

Find a fraction equivalent to the given fraction.

1. $\frac{2}{9}$ ________ 2. $\frac{8}{15}$ ________ 3. $\frac{7}{8}$ ________

4. $\frac{16}{24}$ ________ 5. $\frac{12}{20}$ ________ 6. $\frac{9}{12}$ ________

Determine whether the fractions in each pair are equivalent.

7. $\frac{8}{10}$ and $\frac{12}{15}$ ________ 8. $\frac{6}{8}$ and $\frac{8}{12}$ ________ 9. $\frac{3}{9}$ and $\frac{4}{8}$ ________

10. $\frac{7}{4}$ and $\frac{9}{5}$ ________ 11. $\frac{15}{12}$ and $\frac{20}{16}$ ________ 12. $\frac{15}{9}$ and $\frac{30}{18}$ ________

Write each as a mixed number.

13. $\frac{21}{8}$ ________ 14. $\frac{37}{4}$ ________ 15. $\frac{16}{5}$ ________ 16. $\frac{49}{9}$ ________

Write each as an improper fraction.

17. $8\frac{2}{3}$ ________ 18. $1\frac{7}{12}$ ________ 19. $25\frac{3}{4}$ ________ 20. $7\frac{5}{6}$ ________

21. Maria's desk is $33\frac{3}{4}$ inches long. Write this number as an improper fraction.

____

22. Leon walked $\frac{5}{8}$ mile. Liz walked $\frac{10}{16}$ mile. Did they walk the same distance?

____

Name ______________________ Date ______________ Class ______________

LESSON 2-10

Practice B

Equivalent Fractions and Decimals

Write each fraction as a decimal. Round to the nearest thousandth, if necessary.

1. $\frac{2}{10}$ ________ 2. $\frac{19}{20}$ ________ 3. $\frac{5}{8}$ ________ 4. $\frac{11}{5}$ ________

5. $\frac{19}{6}$ ________ 6. $\frac{17}{4}$ ________ 7. $\frac{13}{12}$ ________ 8. $\frac{30}{7}$ ________

9. $\frac{7}{4}$ ________ 10. $\frac{9}{20}$ ________ 11. $\frac{11}{10}$ ________ 12. $\frac{2}{25}$ ________

Write each decimal as a fraction in simplest form.

13. 0.85 ________ 14. 0.11 ________ 15. –0.25 ________

16. 4.3 ________ 17. 7.75 ________ 18. 5.03 ________

19. –1.06 ________ 20. 0.375 ________ 21. –2.65 ________

22. –5.6 ________ 23. 1.12 ________ 24. 0.005 ________

Write each answer as a decimal rounded to the nearest thousandth.

25. In the 1998 Winter Olympics, a total of 205 medals were awarded. The United States won 13 medals. What portion of the medals did the United States win?

____

26. On a test, Hailey answered 64 out of 75 question correctly. What portion of her answers was correct?

____

Name ______________________ Date ______________ Class ______________

LESSON 2-11

Practice B

Comparing and Ordering Rational Numbers

Compare the fractions. Write < or >.

1. $-\frac{7}{8}$ ____ $-\frac{5}{8}$

2. $\frac{3}{10}$ ____ $\frac{3}{8}$

3. $4\frac{7}{12}$ ____ $5\frac{5}{12}$

4. $\frac{35}{40}$ ____ $\frac{22}{50}$

5. $-\frac{1}{2}$ ____ $\frac{3}{4}$

6. $-3\frac{7}{8}$ ____ $-3\frac{9}{10}$

Compare the decimals. Write < or >.

7. –0.531 ____ –0.513

8. 0.73 ____ 0.073

9. $3.\overline{59}$ ____ 3.599

10. 0.121 ____ 0.12

11. –7.56 ____ –5.76

12. –.099 ____ –.097

Order the numbers from least to greatest.

13. $\frac{4}{9}$, 0.4, 0.45 ______________

14. 1.7, 1.65, $1\frac{2}{3}$ ______________

15. 3.18, $3\frac{1}{8}$, 3.80 ______________

16. –5, –5.25, $-5\frac{2}{5}$ ______________

17. $-6\frac{3}{4}$, 6.34, –6.4 ______________

18. $\frac{11}{12}$, $\frac{8}{9}$, 0.91 ______________

19. $-\frac{3}{5}$, $-\frac{5}{7}$, –0.65 ______________

20. 0.3, 0.345, $\frac{1}{3}$ ______________

21. –0.75, $\frac{7}{8}$, $-\frac{5}{8}$ ______________

22. A ream of paper contains 500 sheets of paper. Norm has 373 sheets of paper left from a ream. Express the portion of a ream Norm has as a fraction and as a decimal.

____

23. The density of Venus, compared to Earth having a density of 1, is 0.943. The density of Mercury is 0.983, compared to the density of Earth. Which planet has a greater density, Venus or Mercury?

____

Name ______________________ Date ______________ Class ______________

LESSON 3-1

Practice B

Estimating with Decimals

Estimate by rounding to the nearest integer.

1. $7.45 + 35.84$ ______________
2. $64.08 - 23.47$ ______________
3. $6.842 + 14.05$ ______________
4. $7.156 + 8.34$ ______________
5. $84.23 + (-78.24)$ ______________
6. $3.78 - 2.078$ ______________
7. $46.47 - 98.75$ ______________
8. $87.24 - 56.38$ ______________
9. $6.324 + 60.324$ ______________
10. $-28.318 + 18.955$ ______________
11. $35.082 + 8.37$ ______________
12. $-62.49 - 12.84$ ______________

Use compatible numbers to estimate.

13. $59.69 \div 19.904$ ______________
14. $86.234 \cdot 9.876$ ______________
15. $54.87 \cdot 19.47$ ______________
16. $-16.04 \cdot 10.45$ ______________
17. $31.25 \cdot 6.57$ ______________
18. $92.67 \div 32.89$ ______________
19. $5.548 \cdot 12.38$ ______________
20. $88.42 \div 7.589$ ______________
21. $90.05 \div 6.21$ ______________

22. Lisha works 20 hours per week at the bowling alley and makes \$8.55 an hour. She gets a raise of \$1.30 an hour. Approximately how much more will she make each week with her raise?

____

23. Miguel is able to save \$87.34 each month. He wants to buy a guitar that costs \$542.45. For about how many months will Miguel have to save before he can buy the guitar?

____

Name ______________________ Date ______________ Class ______________

LESSON 3-2

Practice B

Adding and Subtracting Decimals

Add. Estimate to check whether each answer is reasonable.

1. 6.14 + 8.91
2. 4.51 + 13.08
3. 12.54 + 21.08
4. 34.22 + (–18.5)
5. –10.10 + (–5.9)
6. 6.87 + (–31.6)
7. 9 + 5.68
8. –15.51 + 8.55
9. 36.36 + 54.54

Subtract.

10. 6.23 – 3.62
11. 8.67 – 6.87
12. 28.94 – 9.48
13. 23.57 – 6.84
14. 16.61 – 7.56
15. 32.08 – 12.37
16. 19 – 6.92
17. 42 – 31.89
18. 23 – 21.45
19. 46.2 – 0.27
20. 22 – 18.63
21. 58.9 – 29.58
22. Anna swims the length of the pool in 38.45 seconds and then swims the length of the pool again in 42.38 seconds. What is her total time for 2 lengths of the pool?
23. Po has 2 gerbils named Yip and Yap. Yip weighs 3.62 ounces, and Yap weighs 2.79 ounces. How much heavier is Yip than Yap?

Name ______________________ Date ______________ Class ______________

LESSON 3-3

Practice B

Multiplying Decimals

Multiply.

1. $6 \cdot 0.3$ ________
2. $3 \cdot 0.05$ ________
3. $0.7 \cdot 4$ ________
4. $8 \cdot 6.1$ ________
5. $7.4 \cdot 6$ ________
6. $1.4 \cdot 9$ ________
7. $4.8 \cdot 7$ ________
8. $3 \cdot 8.2$ ________
9. $5.5 \cdot 8$ ________
10. $1.5 \cdot 6$ ________
11. $7.9 \cdot 2$ ________
12. $5 \cdot 6.9$ ________

Multiply. Estimate to check whether each answer is reasonable.

13. $6.3 \cdot 7.8$ ________
14. $9.7 \cdot (-4.7)$ ________
15. $6.8 \cdot 0.9$ ________
16. $2.8 \cdot 8.2$ ________
17. $-7 \cdot 6.42$ ________
18. $1.9 \cdot 7.22$ ________
19. $-5.3 \cdot (-8.4)$ ________
20. $7.16 \cdot 0.03$ ________
21. $1.56 \cdot (-7.8)$ ________
22. $4.6 \cdot 3.1$ ________
23. $0.62 \cdot 1.45$ ________
24. $-5.74 \cdot 1.9$ ________
25. Jordan jogged 4.8 miles each day for 21 days last month. How many miles did she jog last month?

____

Name ______________________ Date ______________ Class ______________

LESSON 3-4

Practice B

Dividing Decimals

Divide.

1. 6 ÷ 0.25 ____________
2. 78.74 ÷ 12.7 ____________
3. 734.8 ÷ –1.67 ____________
4. 56.525 ÷ 0.85 ____________
5. 44.22 ÷ (–6.7) ____________
6. –6.46 ÷ 0.04 ____________

Divide. Estimate to check whether your answer is reasonable.

7. 63 ÷ (–4.5) ____________
8. 8 ÷ 3.2 ____________
9. 87 ÷ 7.25 ____________
10. –36 ÷ 1.6 ____________
11. 42 ÷ 4.8 ____________
12. 90 ÷ 0.36 ____________

13. Freddie used 6.75 gallons of gas to drive 155.25 miles. What was his car's gas mileage? ____________

14. The members of a book club met at a restaurant for dinner. The total bill was $112.95 and they shared the bill equally. Each person paid $12.55. How many members are there in the book club? ____________

Name ______________________ Date ______________ Class ______________

LESSON 3-5

Practice B

Solving Equations Containing Decimals

Solve.

1. $t + 0.77 = 9.3$ ________
2. $p - 1.34 = -11.8$ ________
3. $r + 2.14 = 7.8$ ________
4. $3.65 + e = -1.4$ ________
5. $w - 16.7 = 8.27$ ________
6. $z - 17.2 = 7.13$ ________
7. $p - 67.5 = 24.81$ ________
8. $h + 26.9 = 12.74$ ________
9. $k + 89.2 = -47.62$ ________
10. $x - 0.45 = 5.97$ ________
11. $1.08 + n = 15.72$ ________
12. $y - 6.32 = 0.73$ ________
13. $4.3p = 28.81$ ________
14. $7.7j = 76.23$ ________
15. $3.8g = -104.12$ ________
16. $18.36 = 2.7y$ ________
17. $99.96 = 6.8x$ ________
18. $293.92 = 17.6c$ ________
19. $\frac{e}{7.4} = 6.9$ ________
20. $\frac{f}{12.7} = 15.6$ ________
21. $\frac{d}{9.7} = 20.8$ ________
22. $\frac{w}{-0.2} = 15.4$ ________
23. $\frac{m}{9.8} = 1.7$ ________
24. $\frac{s}{14.35} = -5.2$ ________
25. Jeff paid a flat fee of $269.50 for a year's worth of vet visits for his 4 cats. He made 14 visits during the year. What was the average cost per visit?

____

Name ____________________ Date ____________ Class ____________

LESSON 3-6

Practice B

Estimating with Fractions

Estimate each sum or difference.

1. $\frac{5}{11} + \frac{4}{9}$ ________

2. $\frac{16}{13} + \frac{8}{9}$ ________

3. $\frac{9}{10} - \frac{4}{9}$ ________

4. $1\frac{5}{8} - \frac{4}{7}$ ________

5. $3\frac{7}{8} + \left(-\frac{2}{5}\right)$ ________

6. $\frac{8}{9} - \frac{1}{12}$ ________

7. $4\frac{5}{16} + 2\frac{9}{10}$ ________

8. $11\frac{3}{7} - 5\frac{5}{6}$ ________

9. $7\frac{1}{16} + \left(-\frac{11}{12}\right)$ ________

Estimate each product or quotient.

10. $12\frac{2}{5} \div 5\frac{3}{4}$ ________

11. $7\frac{7}{8} \cdot 4\frac{3}{5}$ ________

12. $5\frac{1}{6} \cdot 3\frac{2}{9}$ ________

13. $23\frac{7}{10} \div 4\frac{2}{5}$ ________

14. $17\frac{11}{12} \div 8\frac{5}{9}$ ________

15. $8\frac{7}{12} \cdot 6\frac{9}{10}$ ________

16. $12\frac{3}{8} \cdot 6\frac{1}{6}$ ________

17. $35\frac{2}{3} \div 3\frac{5}{7}$ ________

18. $16\frac{5}{8} \cdot 2\frac{1}{5}$ ________

19. A hallway has a length of $15\frac{3}{4}$ feet and a width of $4\frac{1}{12}$ feet. Estimate the area of the hallway in square feet.

____

20. A 6-week old puppy weighed $8\frac{7}{16}$ pounds. At 12 weeks of age, the same puppy weighed about $17\frac{3}{8}$ pounds. Estimate how much weight the puppy gained between the ages of 6 weeks and 12 weeks.

____

Name ______________________ Date ______________ Class ______________

LESSON 3-7

Practice B

Adding and Subtracting Fractions

Add or subtract. Write each answer in simplest form.

1. $\frac{1}{5} + \frac{2}{5}$

2. $\frac{4}{15} + \frac{8}{15}$

3. $\frac{7}{12} - \frac{5}{12}$

4. $\frac{9}{10} - \frac{7}{10}$

5. $\frac{7}{12} - \frac{11}{12}$

6. $\frac{2}{7} + \frac{6}{7}$

7. $\frac{11}{15} + \frac{7}{15}$

8. $\frac{3}{16} - \frac{1}{16}$

9. $\frac{8}{21} + \frac{5}{21}$

10. $\frac{4}{5} - \frac{3}{4}$

11. $\frac{3}{8} + \frac{1}{2}$

12. $\frac{2}{5} - \frac{21}{25}$

13. $\frac{11}{12} + \frac{5}{6}$

14. $\frac{7}{8} - \frac{5}{12}$

15. $\frac{9}{10} + \frac{5}{6}$

16. $\frac{2}{5} - \frac{7}{8}$

17. $\frac{5}{6} + \frac{11}{15}$

18. $\frac{3}{4} - \frac{8}{15}$

19. The school track is $\frac{7}{8}$ mile in length. Sherri ran $\frac{2}{3}$ mile. How much farther does she have to go to get all the way around the track?

20. The Millers budget $\frac{1}{2}$ of their income for fixed expenses and $\frac{1}{8}$ of their income for savings. What fraction of their income is left?

Name ____________________ Date ______________ Class ______________

LESSON 3-8

Practice B

Adding and Subtracting Mixed Numbers

Add. Write each answer in simplest form.

1. $7\frac{2}{7} + 6\frac{5}{7}$

2. $5\frac{4}{9} + 3\frac{7}{9}$

3. $4\frac{1}{3} + 8\frac{1}{4}$

4. $2\frac{7}{15} + 3\frac{11}{15}$

5. $6\frac{9}{10} + 1\frac{2}{5}$

6. $2\frac{3}{5} + 1\frac{11}{20}$

7. $5\frac{9}{10} + 2\frac{5}{8}$

8. $2\frac{11}{12} + 3\frac{7}{8}$

9. $1\frac{2}{3} + 5\frac{7}{9}$

Subtract. Write each answer in simplest form.

10. $7\frac{7}{9} - 3\frac{5}{9}$

11. $9\frac{7}{10} - 5\frac{3}{10}$

12. $4\frac{13}{15} - 1\frac{7}{15}$

13. $6\frac{2}{3} - 3\frac{3}{5}$

14. $10\frac{3}{4} - 6\frac{1}{3}$

15. $2\frac{3}{10} - 1\frac{7}{8}$

16. $8\frac{7}{12} - 6\frac{1}{3}$

17. $5\frac{7}{8} - 3\frac{9}{10}$

18. $7\frac{6}{7} - 6\frac{3}{4}$

19. Tucker ran $5\frac{3}{8}$ miles on Monday and $3\frac{3}{4}$ miles on Tuesday. How far did he run on both days?

Name ______________________ Date ______________ Class ______________

LESSON 3-9

Practice B

Multiplying Fractions and Mixed Numbers

Multiply. Write each answer in simplest form.

1. $5 \cdot \frac{1}{2}$ ____________

2. $9 \cdot \frac{3}{4}$ ____________

3. $6 \cdot -\frac{2}{5}$ ____________

4. $\frac{9}{15} \cdot \frac{5}{7}$ ____________

5. $\frac{9}{14} \cdot -\frac{7}{9}$ ____________

6. $\frac{7}{12} \cdot \frac{6}{14}$ ____________

7. $-12 \cdot \frac{3}{7}$ ____________

8. $15 \cdot \frac{5}{6}$ ____________

9. $21 \cdot \frac{3}{8}$ ____________

10. $2\frac{1}{3} \cdot \frac{3}{5}$ ____________

11. $3\frac{2}{5} \cdot \frac{1}{2}$ ____________

12. $4\frac{5}{6} \cdot \frac{2}{5}$ ____________

13. $2\frac{2}{5} \cdot \frac{2}{3}$ ____________

14. $3\frac{3}{4} \cdot \frac{2}{5}$ ____________

15. $8\frac{1}{6} \cdot \frac{3}{7}$ ____________

16. $2\frac{1}{3} \cdot 3\frac{3}{8}$ ____________

17. $1\frac{3}{5} \cdot 6\frac{2}{3}$ ____________

18. $2\frac{2}{5} \cdot 4\frac{5}{6}$ ____________

19. Rolf spent 15 hours last week practicing his saxophone. If $\frac{3}{10}$ of the time was spent practicing warm-up routines, how much time did he spend practicing warm-up routines?

____

20. A muffin recipe calls for $\frac{2}{5}$ tablespoon of vanilla extract for 6 muffins. Arthur is making 18 muffins. How much vanilla extract does he need?

____

Name ______________________ Date ______________ Class ______________

LESSON 3-10

Practice B

Dividing Fractions and Mixed Numbers

Divide. Write each answer in simplest form.

1. $4 \div \frac{1}{2}$ ____________

2. $\frac{1}{5} \div \frac{1}{4}$ ____________

3. $\frac{1}{3} \div \frac{3}{5}$ ____________

4. $\frac{8}{9} \div \frac{2}{3}$ ____________

5. $-\frac{3}{8} \div \frac{3}{4}$ ____________

6. $\frac{7}{10} \div \frac{3}{5}$ ____________

7. $\frac{5}{12} \div \frac{2}{5}$ ____________

8. $\frac{3}{4} \div \frac{4}{9}$ ____________

9. $\frac{7}{12} \div \frac{3}{4}$ ____________

10. $-4\frac{1}{6} \div \frac{1}{3}$ ____________

11. $3\frac{1}{4} \div \frac{2}{5}$ ____________

12. $6\frac{1}{9} \div \frac{1}{6}$ ____________

13. $2\frac{1}{4} \div 1\frac{3}{4}$ ____________

14. $3\frac{3}{4} \div 2\frac{5}{6}$ ____________

15. $5\frac{1}{3} \div -1\frac{4}{5}$ ____________

16. $2\frac{1}{2} \div 2\frac{1}{3}$ ____________

17. $-1\frac{3}{4} \div 1\frac{1}{4}$ ____________

18. $7\frac{2}{3} \div 1\frac{1}{5}$ ____________

19. Burger Barn has $46\frac{2}{3}$ pounds of ground beef. How many $\frac{1}{3}$-pound burgers can be made using all the ground beef?

____

20. Roberto needs some roofing tiles to be cut from a large tile. How many tiles that are each $14\frac{3}{8}$ inches in length can he cut from a larger piece of tile that is $100\frac{5}{8}$ inches long?

____

Name ______________________ Date ______________ Class ______________

LESSON 3-11

Practice B

Solving Equations Containing Fractions

Solve. Write each answer in simplest form.

1. $t - \frac{3}{7} = \frac{4}{7}$ ______

2. $g - \frac{5}{16} = \frac{3}{16}$ ______

3. $k - \frac{3}{10} = \frac{2}{5}$ ______

4. $n + \frac{1}{7} = \frac{2}{3}$ ______

5. $j + \frac{5}{6} = \frac{17}{18}$ ______

6. $f + \frac{5}{12} = \frac{3}{4}$ ______

7. $\frac{1}{4}s = \frac{3}{4}$ ______

8. $\frac{1}{5}a = \frac{1}{2}$ ______

9. $\frac{4}{5}h = \frac{8}{9}$ ______

10. $p - \frac{2}{3} = \frac{5}{8}$ ______

11. $d - \frac{3}{5} = \frac{7}{10}$ ______

12. $y - \frac{2}{7} = 3\frac{1}{4}$ ______

13. $c + \frac{5}{12} = 2\frac{1}{6}$ ______

14. $w + \frac{4}{15} = 3\frac{1}{3}$ ______

15. $z + \frac{6}{7} = 2\frac{3}{5}$ ______

16. $\frac{5}{6}m = \frac{8}{9}$ ______

17. $\frac{1}{2}x = 3\frac{7}{15}$ ______

18. $\frac{1}{5}r = 2\frac{2}{3}$ ______

19. Sarabeth ran $1\frac{2}{5}$ miles on a path around the park. This was $\frac{5}{8}$ of the distance around the park. What is the distance around the park?

______

20. An interior decorator bought $12\frac{1}{2}$ yards of material to make drapes. He used $8\frac{2}{3}$ yards on 1 pair of drapes. How much material does he have left?

______

Name ______________________ Date ______________ Class ______________

LESSON 4-1

Practice B

Ratios

The annual dog show has 22 collies, 28 boxers, and 18 poodles. Write each ratio in all three forms.

1. collies to poodles

____

2. boxers to collies

____

3. poodles to boxers

____

4. poodles to collies

____

The Franklin School District has 15 art teachers, 27 math teachers, and 18 Spanish teachers. Write the given ratio in all three forms.

5. art teachers to math teachers

____

6. math teachers to Spanish teachers

____

7. Spanish teachers to all teachers

____

8. art and math teachers to Spanish teachers

____

9. Thirty-two students are asked whether the school day should be longer. Twenty-four vote “no” and 8 vote “yes.” Write the ratio of “no” votes to “yes” votes in simplest form.

____

10. A train car has 64 seats. There are 48 passengers on the train. Write the ratio of seats to passengers in simplest form.

____

11. Tell whose CD collection has the greater ratio of rock CDs to total CDs.

____

	Glen	Nina
Classical CDs	4	8
Rock CDs	9	12
Other CDs	5	7

Name ______________________ Date ______________ Class ______________

LESSON 4-2

Practice B

Rates

1. A part-time job pays $237.50 for 25 hours of work. How much money does the job pay per hour? ______________

2. A class trip consists of 84 students and 6 teachers. How many students per teacher are there? ______________

3. A factory builds 960 cars in 5 days. What is the average number of cars the factory produces per day? ______________

4. The Wireless Cafe charges $5.40 for 45 minutes of Internet access. How much money does The Wireless Cafe charge per minute? ______________

5. A bowler scores 3,152 points in 16 games. What is his average score in points per game? ______________

6. Melissa drives 238 miles in 5 hours. What is her average rate of speed? ______________

7. An ocean liner travels 1,233 miles in 36 hours. What is the ocean liner's average rate of speed? ______________

8. A plane is scheduled to complete a 1,792-mile flight in 3.5 hours. In order to complete the trip on time, what should be the plane's average rate of speed? ______________

9. The Nuthouse sells macadamia nuts in three sizes. The 12 oz jar sells for $8.65, the 16 oz jar sells for $10.99, and the 24 oz gift tin costs $16.99. Which size costs less per ounce? ______________

Name ______________________ Date ______________ Class ______________

LESSON 4-3

Practice B

Identifying and Writing Proportions

Determine whether the ratios are proportional.

1. $\frac{3}{4}, \frac{24}{32}$ ______________

2. $\frac{5}{6}, \frac{15}{18}$ ______________

3. $\frac{10}{12}, \frac{20}{32}$ ______________

4. $\frac{7}{10}, \frac{22}{30}$ ______________

5. $\frac{9}{6}, \frac{21}{14}$ ______________

6. $\frac{7}{9}, \frac{24}{27}$ ______________

7. $\frac{4}{10}, \frac{6}{15}$ ______________

8. $\frac{7}{12}, \frac{13}{20}$ ______________

9. $\frac{4}{9}, \frac{6}{12}$ ______________

10. $\frac{7}{8}, \frac{14}{16}$ ______________

11. $\frac{9}{10}, \frac{45}{50}$ ______________

12. $\frac{3}{7}, \frac{10}{21}$ ______________

Find a ratio equivalent to each ratio. Then use the ratios to write a proportion.

13. $\frac{7}{9}$ ______________

14. $\frac{11}{12}$ ______________

15. $\frac{14}{15}$ ______________

16. $\frac{35}{55}$ ______________

17. $\frac{14}{10}$ ______________

18. $\frac{25}{18}$ ______________

Name ______________________ Date ______________ Class ______________

LESSON 4-4

Practice B

Solving Proportions

Use cross products to solve each proportion.

1. $\frac{2}{5} = \frac{x}{35}$ ______

2. $\frac{7}{r} = \frac{1}{4}$ ______

3. $\frac{k}{75} = \frac{9}{15}$ ______

4. $\frac{1}{3} = \frac{z}{27}$ ______

5. $\frac{2}{11} = \frac{12}{d}$ ______

6. $\frac{24}{s} = \frac{4}{12}$ ______

7. $\frac{w}{42} = \frac{6}{7}$ ______

8. $\frac{t}{54} = \frac{2}{9}$ ______

9. $\frac{3}{8} = \frac{a}{64}$ ______

10. $\frac{17}{34} = \frac{7}{f}$ ______

11. $\frac{15}{h} = \frac{5}{6}$ ______

12. $\frac{4}{15} = \frac{36}{c}$ ______

13. $\frac{z}{25} = \frac{12}{5}$ ______

14. $\frac{36}{k} = \frac{9}{4}$ ______

15. $\frac{5}{14} = \frac{n}{42}$ ______

16. $\frac{8}{9} = \frac{40}{m}$ ______

17. $\frac{7}{c} = \frac{63}{54}$ ______

18. $\frac{24}{21} = \frac{s}{35}$ ______

19. $\frac{e}{22} = \frac{6}{15}$ ______

20. $\frac{3}{v} = \frac{12}{17}$ ______

21. $\frac{5}{14} = \frac{4}{a}$ ______

22. Eight oranges cost $1.00. How much will 5 dozen oranges cost?

____

23. A recipe calls for 2 eggs to make 10 pancakes. How many eggs will you need to make 35 pancakes?

____

Name ______________________ Date ______________ Class ______________

LESSON 4-5

Practice B

Customary Measurements

Choose the most appropriate customary unit for each measurement.
Justify your answer.

1. the weight of a paperback book

____

____

2. the capacity of a large soup pot

____

____

3. the length of a dining room table

____

____

4. the weight of an elephant

____

____

Convert each measure.

5. 6 mi to feet _______________

6. 104 oz to pounds _______________

7. 12 qt to pints _______________

8. 5,000 lb to tons _______________

9. 48 yd to feet _______________

10. 96 fl oz to pints _______________

11. 6.5 ft to inches _______________

12. 20 qt to gallons _______________

13. $3\frac{1}{4}$ lb to ounces _______________

14. Marina has 2.5 lb of cashews. She puts 6 oz of cashews in a bag and gives the bag to her brother. What weight of cashews does Marina have left?

____

15. Faye is 5 ft 5 in. Faye is 10 in. shorter than her older brother. How tall is Faye's older brother?

____

Name ______________________ Date ______________ Class ______________

LESSON 4-6

Practice B

Metric Measurements

Choose the most appropriate metric unit for each measurement. Justify your answer.

1. The capacity of a paper cup

2. The mass of a small poodle.

3. The width of a computer screen

4. The mass of a pencil

Convert each measure.

5. 496 mm to centimeters

6. 0.68 kg to grams

7. 3,800 mL to liters

8. 832 mg to grams

9. 76 km to meters

10. 2.9 cm to meters

11. 0.041 kL to liters

12. 14.9 g to milligrams

13. 7,800 cm to meters

14. Sam's laptop computer has a mass of 4.2 kg. Fred's laptop computer has a mass of 4,940 grams. Which computer has the lesser mass? Explain your answer.

15. Elise makes a poster that is 1.5 m tall. Meg makes a poster that is 96 cm tall. Who makes a taller poster? Explain your answer.

Name ______________________ Date ______________ Class ______________

LESSON 4-7

Practice B

Dimensional Analysis

1. David takes 300 milligrams of medicine every day. Find this rate in grams per day.

____

2. Jody runs the 500-yard dash for his school's track team in 1 minute. Find this rate in yards per second.

____

3. Sean drinks six 12-fluid ounce cans of soda a week. Find this rate in pints per week.

____

4. One quart is about 0.946 liters. A recipe for punch requires diluting the punch concentrate with 7 quarts of water. To the nearest tenth, how many liters of water are required to dilute the concentrate according to the directions?

____

5. One pound is about 0.454 kilograms. Jesse's dog Angel weighs $18\frac{1}{2}$ pounds. To the nearest tenth, how many kilograms does Angel weigh?

____

6. One mile is about 1.61 kilometers. The volcano Mauna Kea is 120 km wide. What is the width of the volcano in miles, rounded to the nearest tenth of a mile?

____

7. A 1-pound weight has a mass of about 0.45 kilograms. A car weighs 2100 pounds. What is the mass of the car in kilograms, rounded to the nearest tenth of a kilogram?

____

8. Tyler is riding his bike from his house to the store, which is 4 miles away. Tyler gets to the store 18 minutes after he leaves his house. Find Tyler's speed in miles per minute. Use dimensional analysis to check the reasonableness of your answer.

____

Name ______________________ Date ______________ Class ______________

LESSON 4-8

Practice B

Similar Figures and Proportions

Tell whether the triangles are similar.

1.

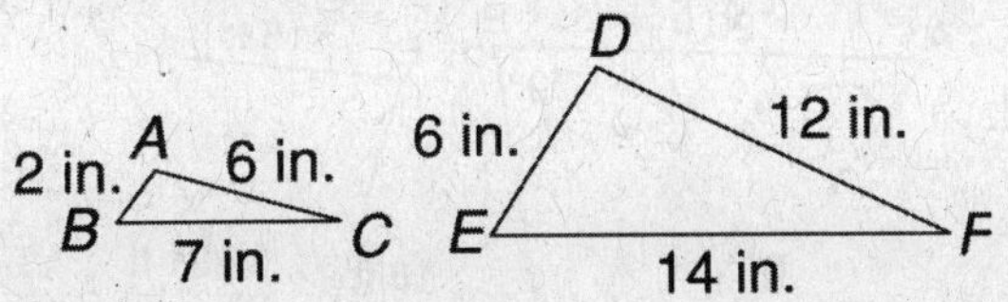

____

____

2.

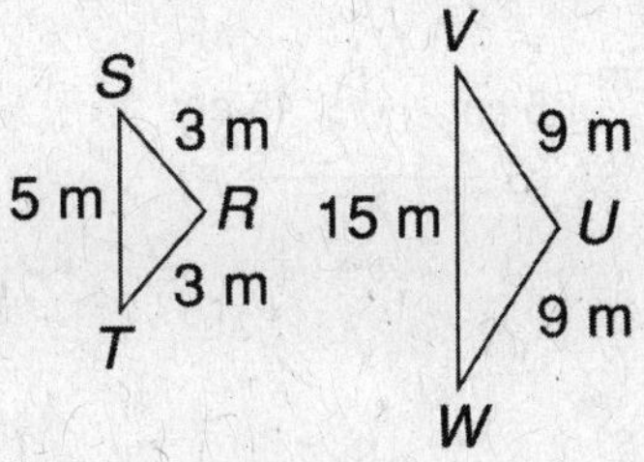

____

____

3.

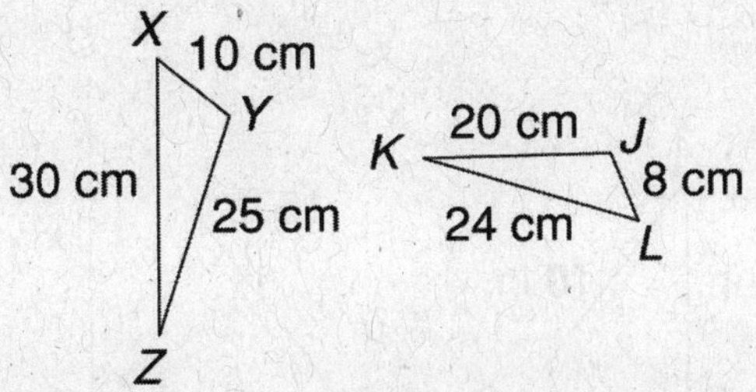

____

____

4.

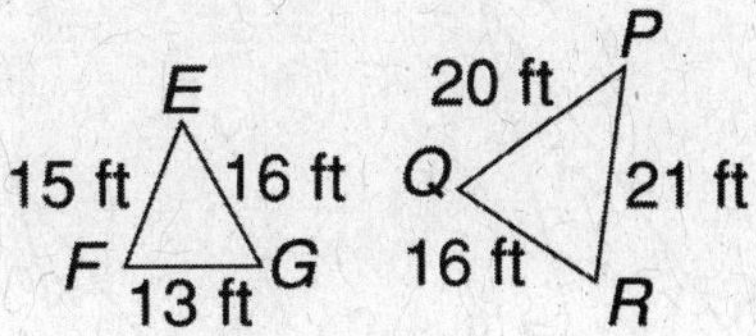

____

____

Tell whether the figures are similar.

5.

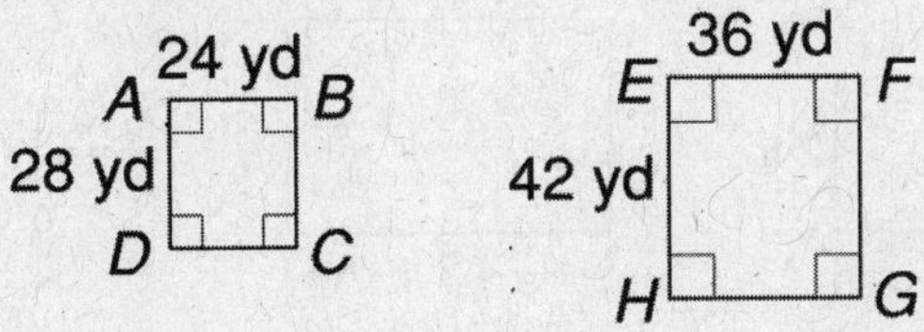

____

____

6.

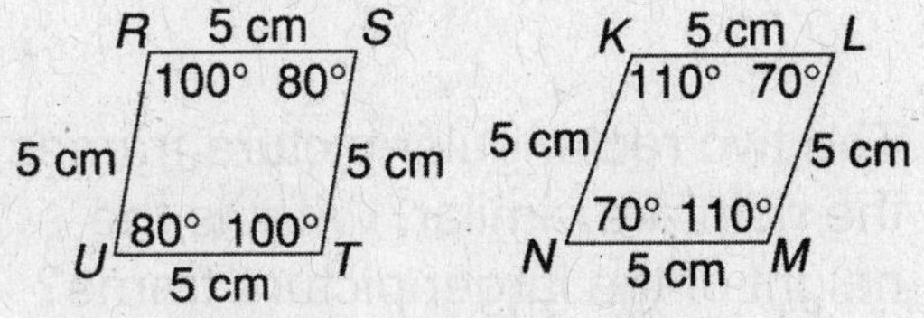

____

____

Name ______________________ Date ______________ Class ______________

LESSON 4-9

Practice B

Using Similar Figures

$\triangle ABC \sim \triangle DEF$ in each pair. Find the unknown measures.

1.

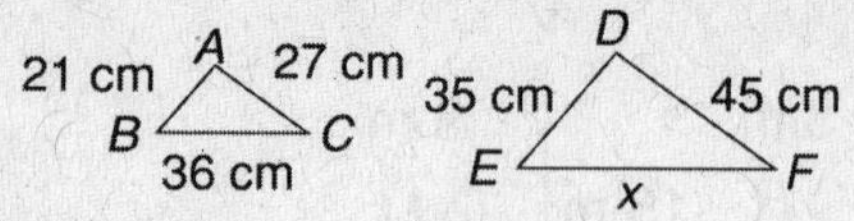

____

2.

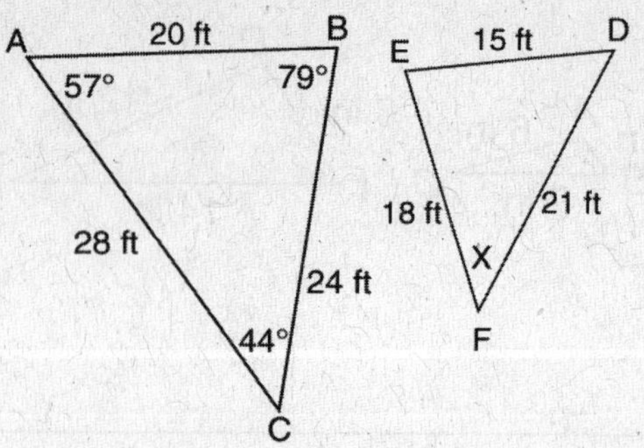

____

3.

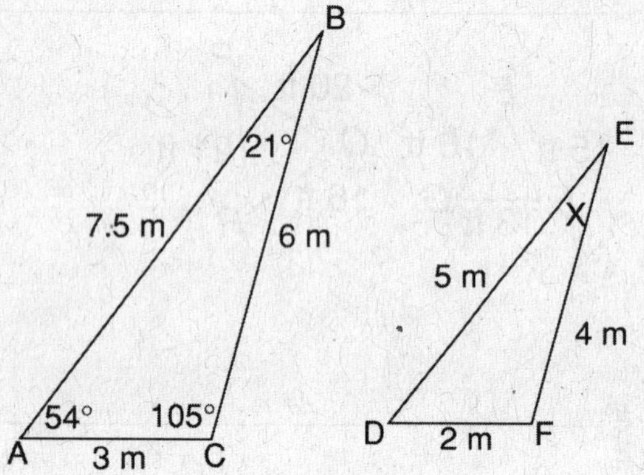

____

4.

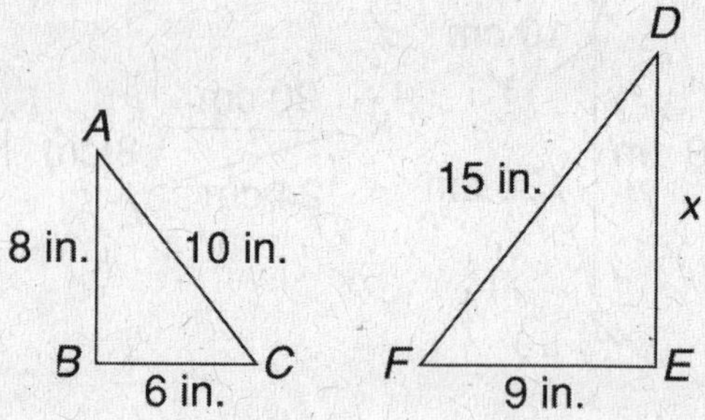

____

5. The two rectangular picture frames at the right are similar. What is the height of the larger picture frame?

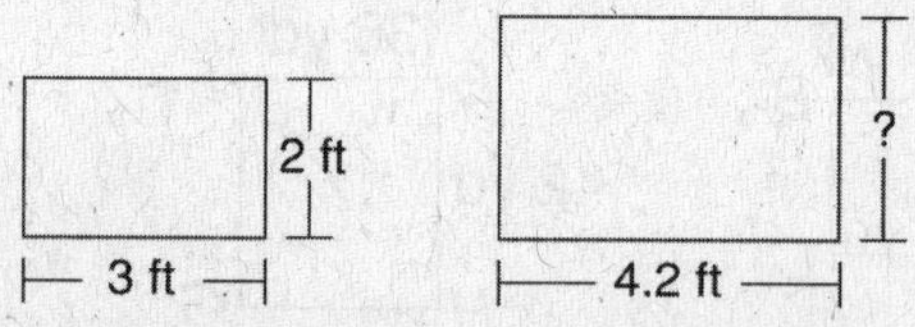

____

6. A palm tree casts a shadow that is 44 feet long. A 6-foot ladder casts a shadow that is 16 feet long. Estimate the height of the palm tree.

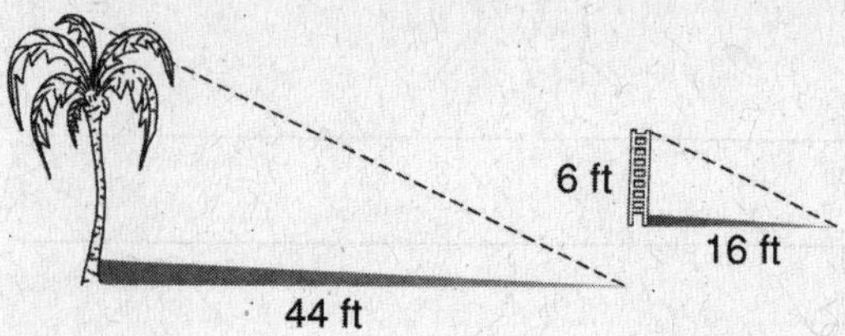

____

Name ____________________ Date ____________ Class ____________

LESSON 4-10

Practice B

Scale Drawings and Scale Models

Identify the scale factor.

1.

	Alligator	**Toy Alligator**
Length (in.)	175	7

____

2.

	Airplane	**Model**
Length (ft)	24	3

____

3.

	Car	**Toy Car**
Length (ft.)	13.5	1.5

____

4.

	Person	**Action Figure**
Height (in.)	66	6

____

5.

	Boat	**Model**
Length (in.)	128	8

____

6.

	Fish	**Fishing Lure**
Length (in.)	18	2

____

7.

	Tiger	**Stuffed Animal**
Length (in.)	70	14

____

8.

	House	**Dollhouse**
Height (ft)	39.2	2.8

____

9. On a scale drawing, a school is 1.6 feet tall. The scale factor is $\frac{1}{22}$. Find the height of the school. ____________

10. On a road map of Pennsylvania, the distance from Philadelphia to Washington, D.C., is 6.8 centimeters. The map scale is 2 cm:40 mi. What is the actual distance between the cities? ____________

11. On a scale drawing, a bicycle is $6\frac{4}{5}$ inches tall. The scale factor is $\frac{1}{6}$. Find the height of the bicycle. ____________

Name ______________________ Date ______________ Class ______________

LESSON 5-1

Practice B

The Coordinate Plane

Identify the quadrant that contains each point.

1. *A* ______________
2. *B* ______________
3. *C* ______________
4. *D* ______________

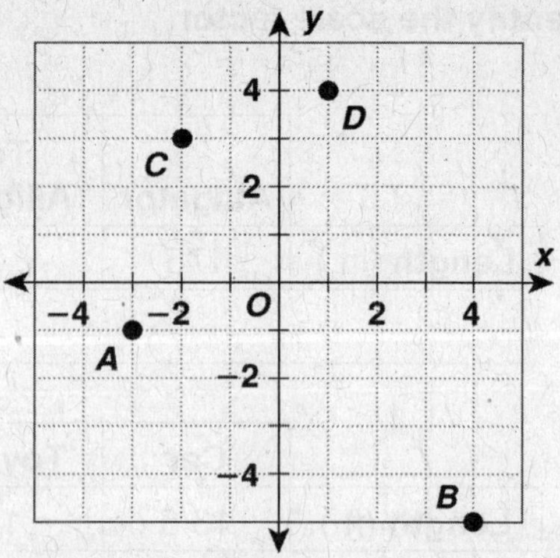

Plot each point on a coordinate plane.

5. (–4, 0)
6. (3, –3)
7. (1, 4)
8. (–5, –1)
9. (–2, 2)
10. (–1, –4)

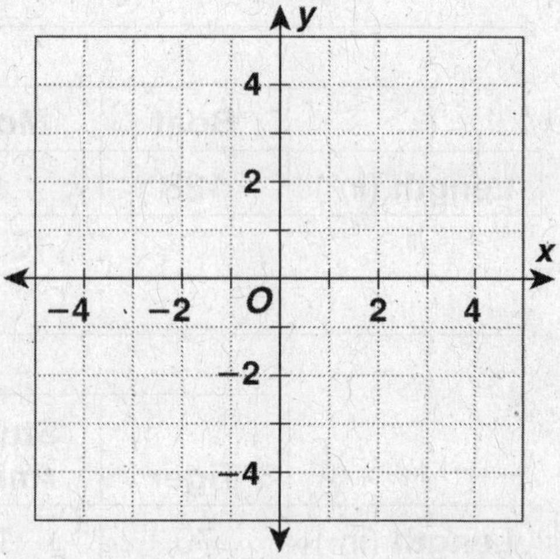

Give the coordinates of each point.

11. *P* ______________
12. *Q* ______________
13. *R* ______________
14. *S* ______________
15. *T* ______________
16. *U* ______________
17. *W* ______________
18. *X* ______________

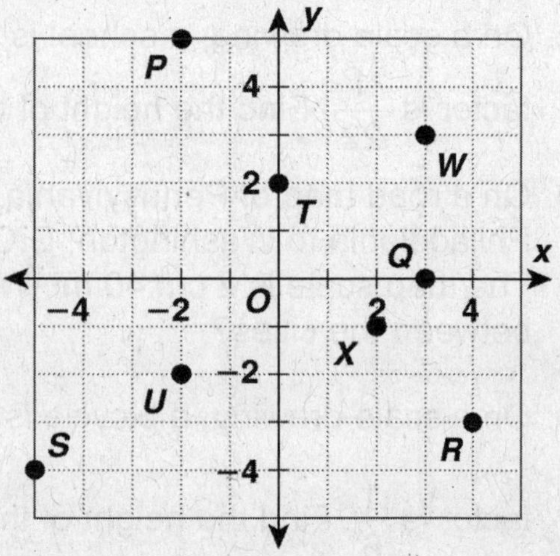

Name ______________________ Date ______________ Class ______________

LESSON 5-2

Practice B

Interpreting Graphs

1. The gas tank in Karen's car was full. Karen drove the car until only $\frac{1}{4}$ of the tank was full. Karen filled up the tank again and drove the car until $\frac{1}{4}$ of the tank was full. Which graph best shows the story? Circle the letter of your answer.

A
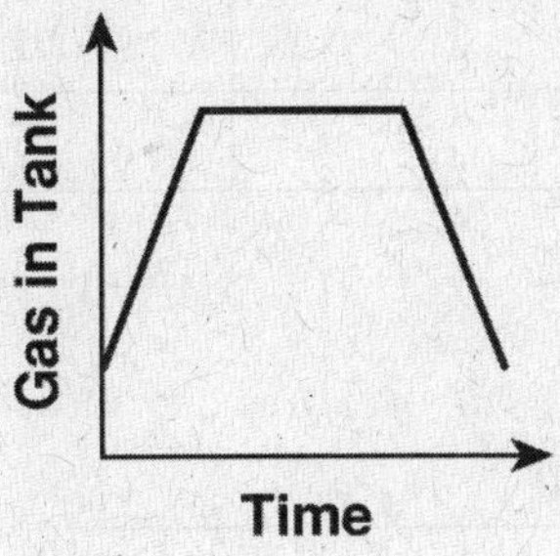

B
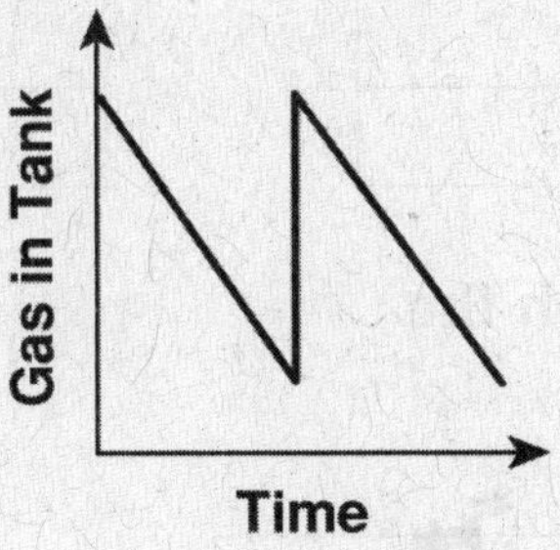

C
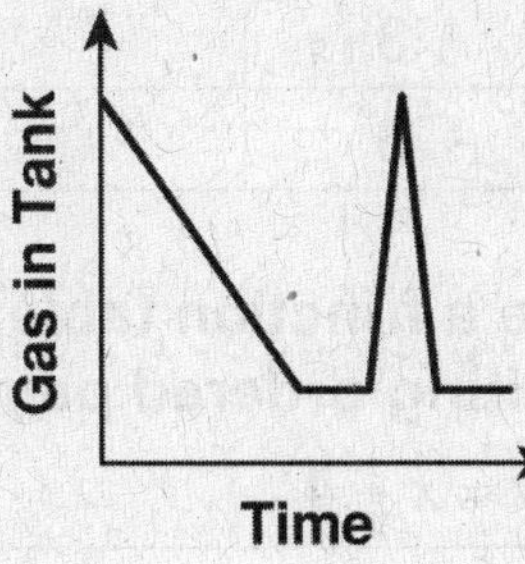

2. An elevator started at the ground floor. It went up to the sixth floor and stopped, then went to the fourth floor and stopped, and finally returned to the ground floor. Which graph best shows the story? Circle the letter of your answer.

F
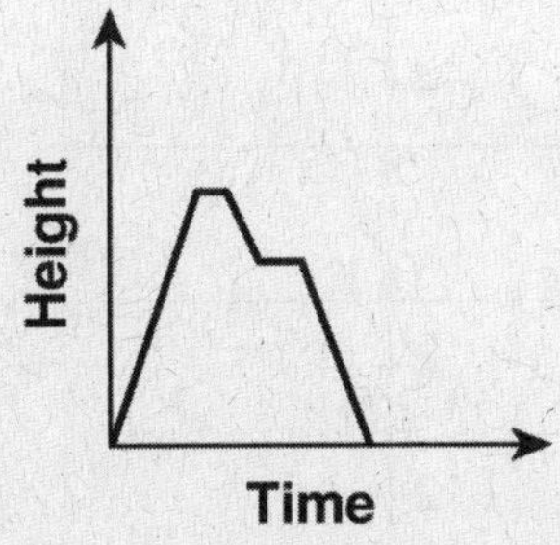

G
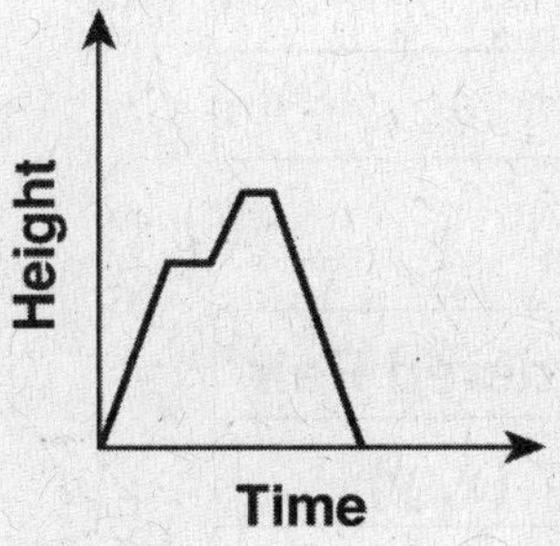

H
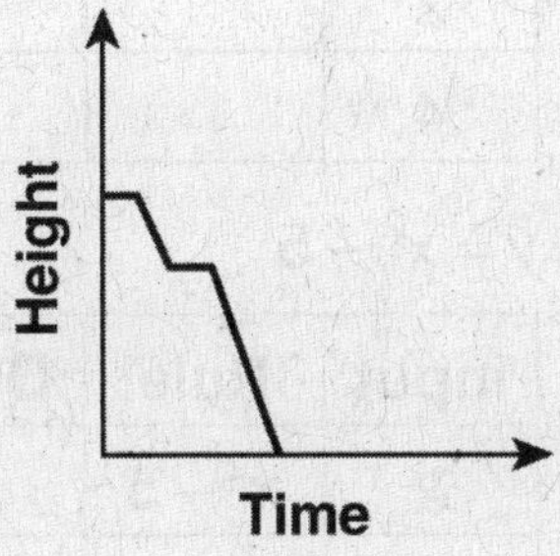

3. Maxine biked 6 miles from her house to the park. She played some softball. Then she biked 4 miles farther to the movie theater. After watching a movie, Maxine returned home. Complete the graph so that it shows the distance Maxine is from home compared to the time.

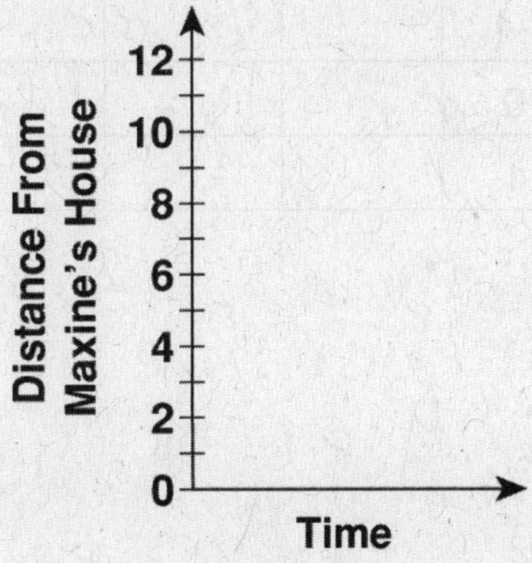

4. Use your graph to find the total number of miles Maxine biked.

____

Name ______________________ Date ______________ Class ______________

LESSON 5-3

Practice B

Functions, Tables, and Graphs

Find the output for each input.

1. $y = 5x - 1$

Input	Rule	Output
x	$5x - 1$	y
–2		
0		
3		
6		

2. $y = -2x^2$

Input	Rule	Output
x	$-2x^2$	y
–2		
2		
3		
4		

Make a function table, and graph the resulting ordered pairs.

3. $y = x \div 4$

Input	Rule	Output	Ordered Pair
x	$x \div 4$	y	(x, y)
–4			
0			
2			
4			

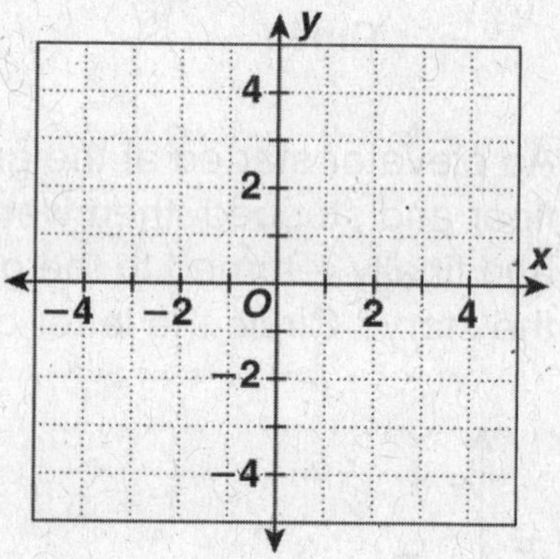

4. $y = x^2 - 5$

Input	Rule	Output	Ordered Pair
x	$x^2 - 5$	y	(x, y)
–2			
–1			
0			
1			

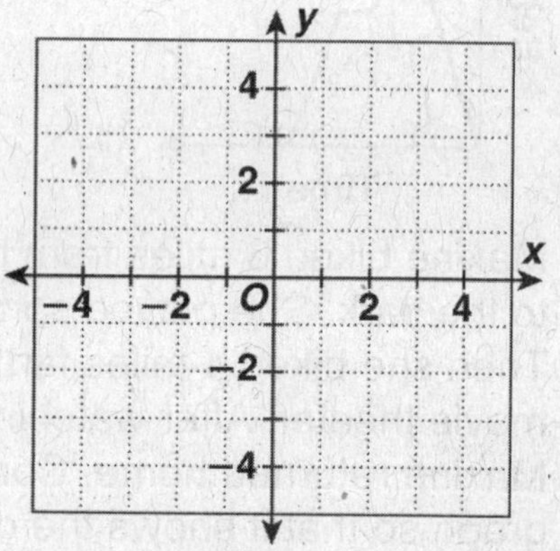

Name ______________________ Date ______________ Class ______________

LESSON 5-4

Practice B

Sequences

Tell whether each sequence of *y*-values is arithmetic or geometric. Then find *y* when *n* = 5.

1.

n	1	2	3	4	5
y	–5	10	25	40	■

____

2.

n	1	2	3	4	5
y	14	28	56	112	■

____

3.

n	1	2	3	4	5
y	4	12	36	108	■

____

4.

n	1	2	3	4	5
y	28	42	56	70	■

____

Write a function that describes each sequence.

5. 12, 24, 36, 48, ...

____

6. 13, 14, 15, 16, ...

____

7. –8, –7, –6, –5, ...

____

8. 2.5, 3.5, 4.5, 5.5, ...

____

9. 9, 18, 27, 36, ...

____

10. –12, –11, –10, –9, ...

____

11. $\frac{3}{4}, 1\frac{3}{4}, 2\frac{3}{4}, 3\frac{3}{4}, \ldots$

____

12. –3, –6, –9, –12, ...

____

13. Mike ran 4 km on Sunday, 6 km on Monday, and 8 km on Tuesday. Write a function that describes the sequence. Then use the function to predict how many kilometers Mike will run on Friday.

____

Name ________________ Date ________ Class ________

LESSON 5-5

Practice B

Graphing Linear Functions

Graph each linear function.

1. $y = -x - 5$

Input	Linear Equation	Output	Ordered Pair
x	$y = -x - 5$	y	(x, y)
−4			
−2			
0			

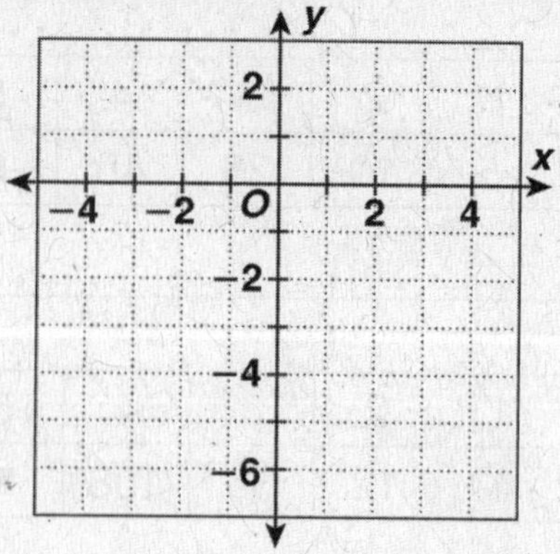

2. $y = 2x - 1$

Input	Linear Equation	Output	Ordered Pair
x	$y = 2x - 1$	y	(x, y)
−2			
0			
1			

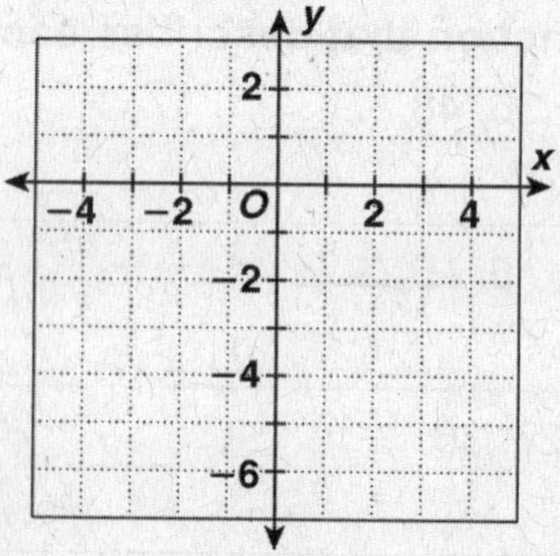

3. The temperature of a swimming pool is 75 °F. When the pool heater is turned on, the temperature rises 2 °F every hour. What will the temperature be after 3 hours? Make a function table to answer the question.

____

4. Mel's Pizza Place charges $15.00 for a large cheese pizza plus $1.25 for each additional topping. What will be the cost of a large pizza with 3 additional toppings? Make a function table to answer the question.

____

Name ______________________ Date ______________ Class ______________

LESSON 5-6

Practice B

Slope and Rates of Change

Tell whether the slope is positive or negative. Then find the slope.

1.

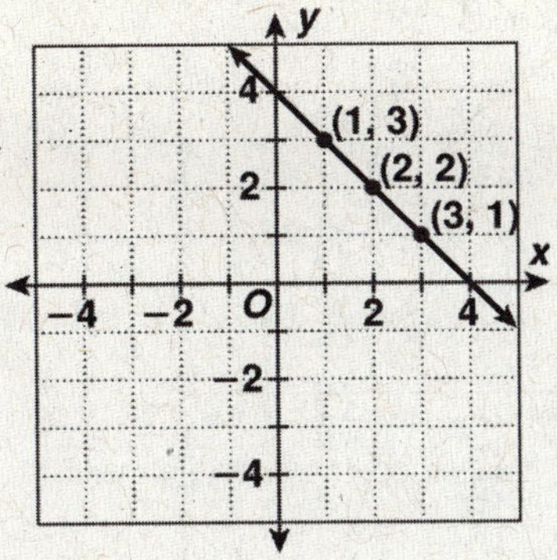

____

2.

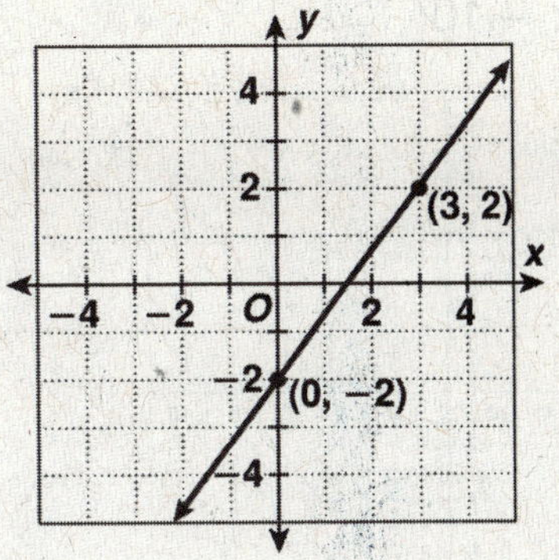

____

Use the given slope and point to graph each line.

3. $-\frac{1}{2}$; (2, 4)

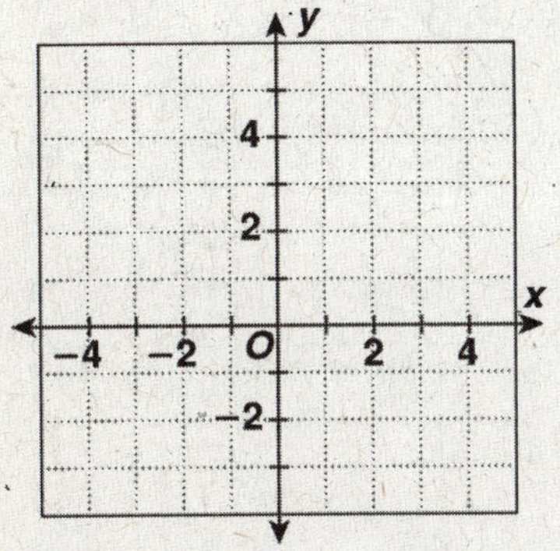

4. $\frac{1}{3}$; (−1, −2)

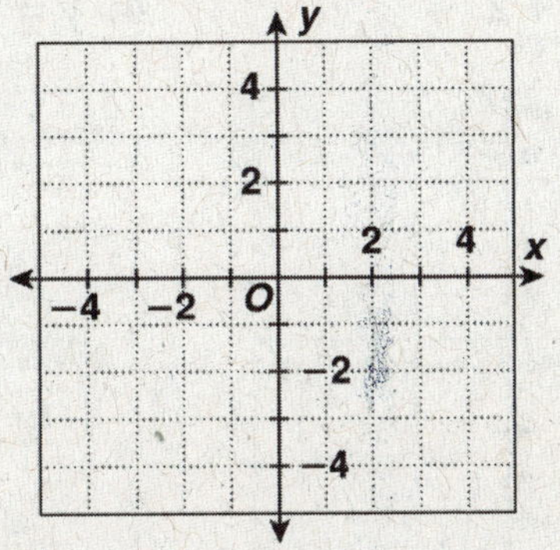

Tell whether each graph shows a constant or variable rate of change.

5.

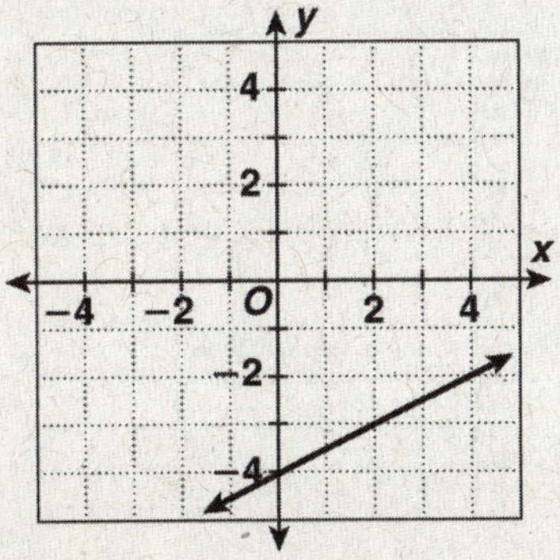

____

6.

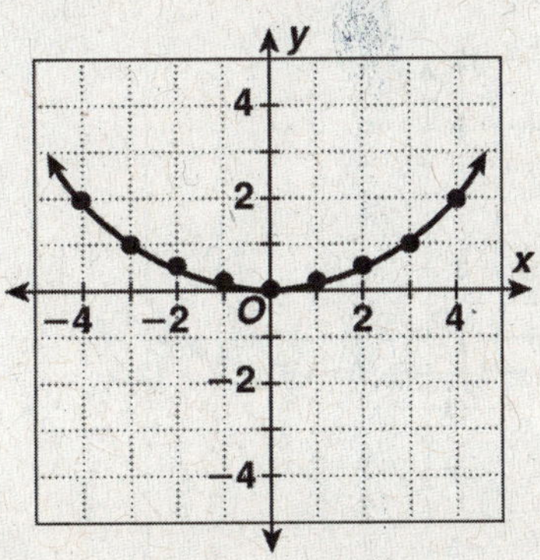

____

Name ______________________ Date ______________ Class ______________

LESSON 5-7

Practice B

Slope-Intercept Form

Find the *x*- and *y*-intercepts.

1. $y = 1\frac{1}{4}x - 10$

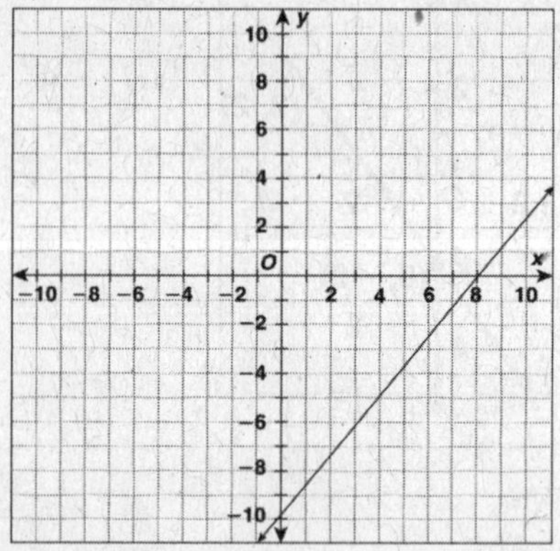

____

2. $y = -2\frac{2}{3}x + 8$

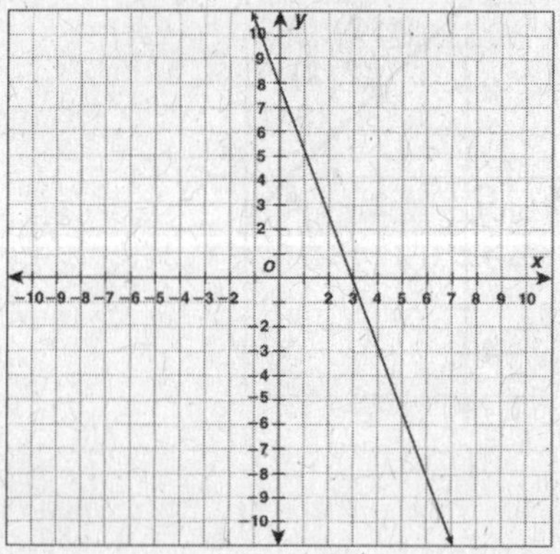

____

Graph each equation.

3. $y = 1\frac{1}{3}x + 2$

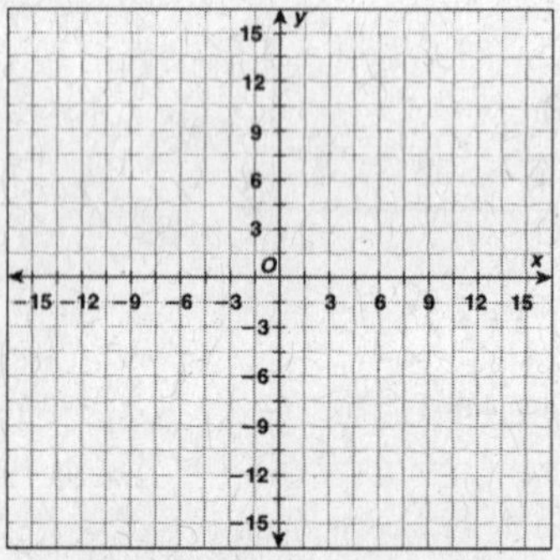

4. $y = x - \frac{1}{2}$

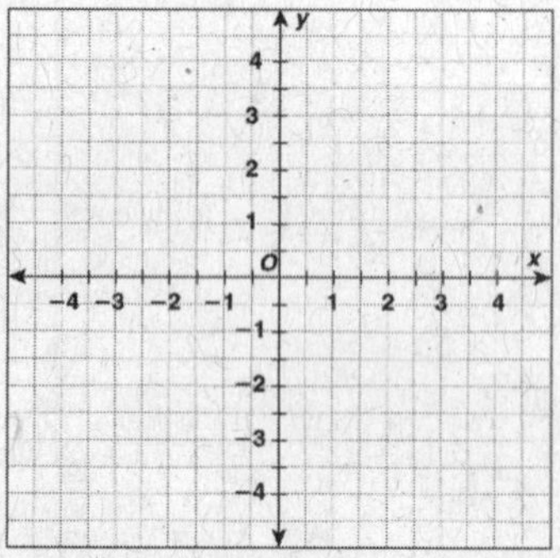

5. $y = -1\frac{3}{7}x + 9$

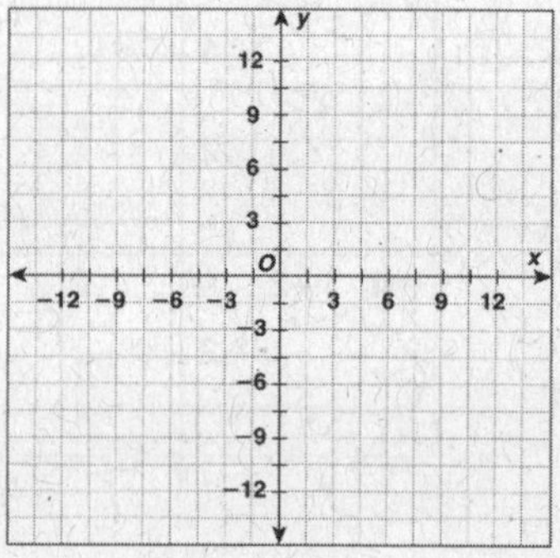

Write the equation of the line in slope-intercept form.

6.

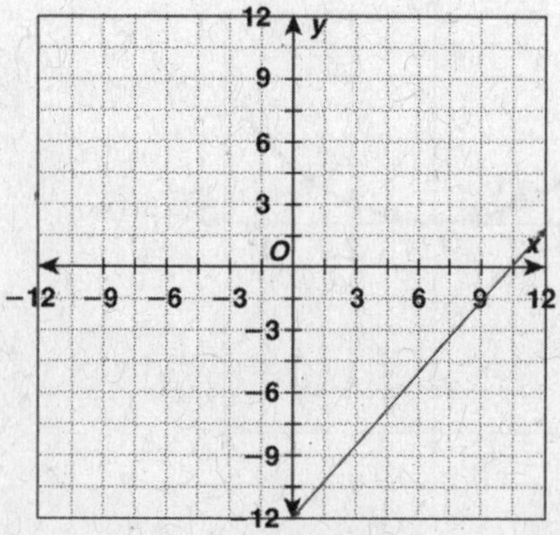

____

7.

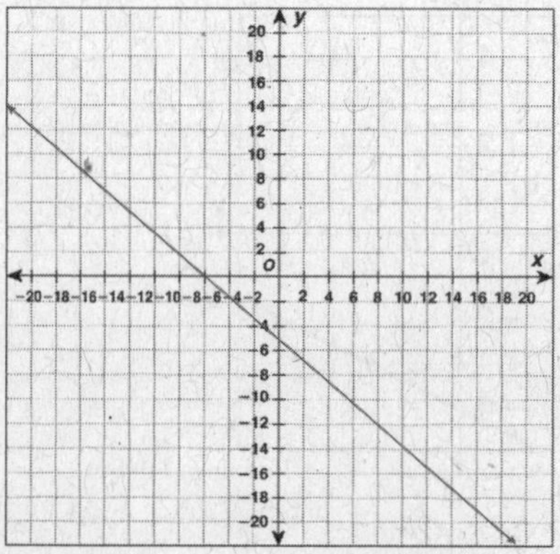

____

Name ______________________ Date ____________ Class ____________

LESSON 5-8

Practice B

Direct Variation

Tell whether each equation represents a direct variation. If so, identify the constant of variation.

1. $y = 7x$

2. $y = 0.04x$

3. $3y = 2x + 5$

4. $y = 13x + 0$

5. $4y = 2x$

6. $8y = 4x - 12$

Tell whether each set of data represents a direct variation. If so, identify the constant of variation and then write the direct variation equation.

7.

x	10	20	30
y	2	4	6

8.

x	2	4	6
y	5	10	15

9.

Times at Bat	3	6	12
Hits	1	2	4

10.

x	–2	8	14
y	3	6	9

11.

School days	18	36	54
Days Roy was out sick	2.5	6	7

12.

Time (Days)	1	1.3	1.6
Distance (k)	640	870	1,095

Tell whether each graph represents a direct variation. If so, identify the constant of variation and then write the direct variation equation.

13.

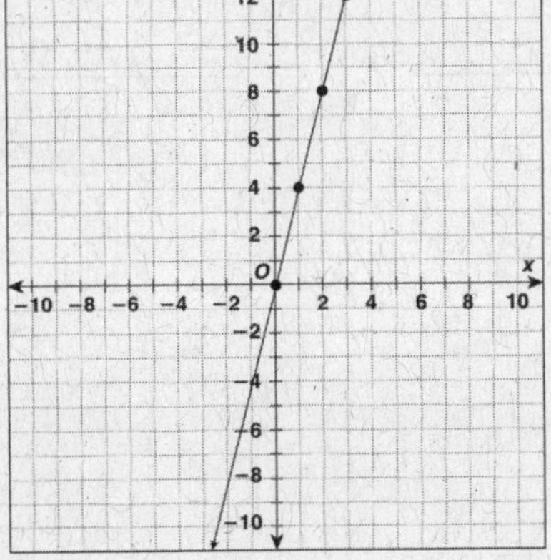

14.

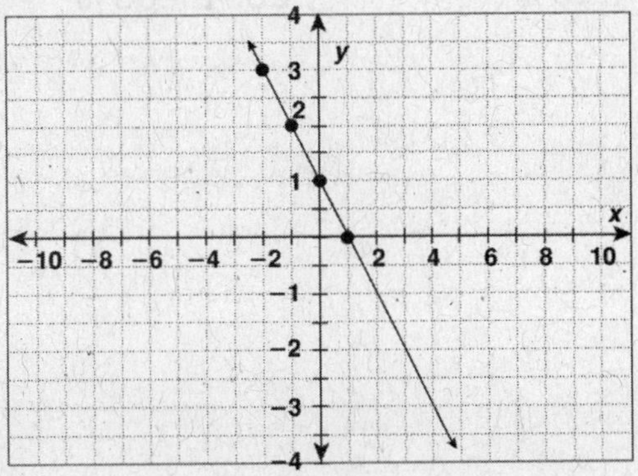

Name ______________________ Date ____________ Class ____________

LESSON 6-1

Practice B

Percents

Write the percent modeled by each grid.

1. 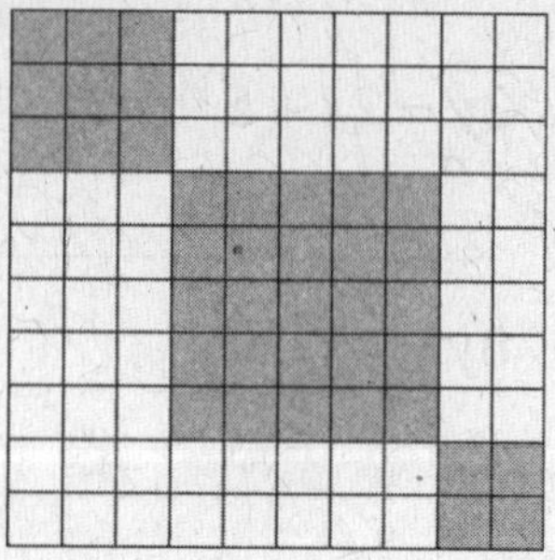

____

2. 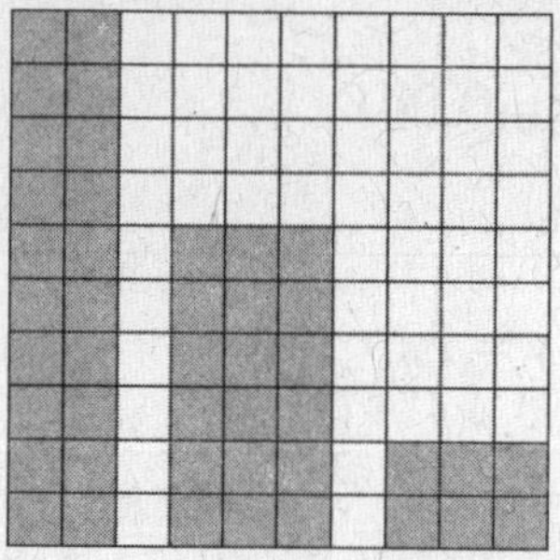

____

3. 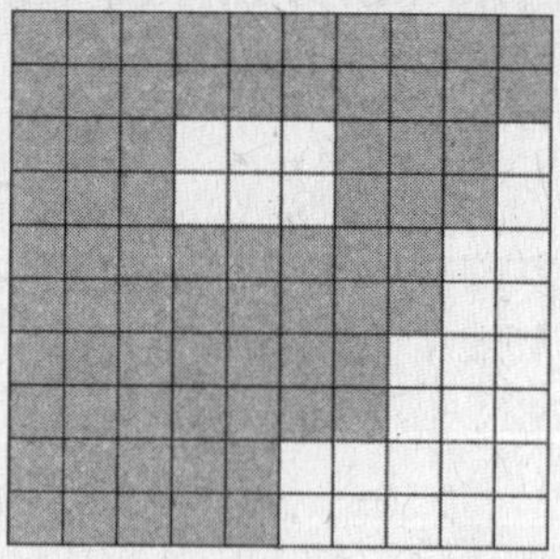

____

Write each percent as a fraction in simplest form.

4. 16% ________
5. 49% ________
6. 20% ________
7. 15% ________
8. 18% ________
9. 60% ________
10. 35% ________
11. 46% ________
12. 86% ________
13. 79% ________
14. 56% ________
15. 45% ________

Write each percent as a decimal.

16. 33% ________
17. 57% ________
18. 46% ________
19. 6% ________
20. 4.7% ________
21. 13.2% ________
22. 75.8% ________
23. 4% ________
24. 1.16% ________
25. 27.05% ________
26. 93.01% ________
27. 7.9% ________

Name ____________ Date ____________ Class ____________

LESSON 6-2

Practice B

Fractions, Decimals, and Percents

Write each decimal as a percent.

1. 0.17 ________
2. 0.56 ________
3. 0.04 ________
4. 0.7 ________
5. 0.025 ________
6. 0.803 ________
7. 0.3 ________
8. 0.072 ________

Write each fraction as a percent.

9. $\frac{13}{40}$ ________
10. $\frac{3}{5}$ ________
11. $\frac{3}{20}$ ________
12. $\frac{5}{12}$ ________
13. $\frac{5}{16}$ ________
14. $\frac{3}{80}$ ________
15. $\frac{5}{6}$ ________
16. $\frac{19}{25}$ ________

Order the numbers from least to greatest.

17. 0.3, $\frac{19}{40}$, 22% ________
18. 11%, $\frac{1}{11}$, $\frac{2}{19}$ ________
19. $\frac{5}{8}$, 0.675, 5.8% ________
20. −0.35, 0.051, −21%
21. $\frac{1}{9}$, 0.351, 27%
22. 0.08, $-\frac{4}{5}$, 0.8

Decide whether pencil and paper, mental math, or a calculator is most useful when solving the following problem. Then solve.

23. The police use a speed gun to monitor one part of a highway. During one hour, 6 out of 25 cars were traveling above the speed limit. What percent of the cars were traveling above the speed limit?

____

____

Name ______________________ Date ______________ Class ______________

LESSON 6-3

Practice B

Estimating with Percents

Use a fraction to estimate the percent of each number.

1. 21% of 82 ________
2. 35% of 42 ________
3. 47% of 164 ________
4. 9% of 68 ________
5. 65% of 78 ________
6. 11% of 92 ________
7. 26% of 124 ________
8. 89% of 51 ________
9. 77% of 198 ________
10. 5% of 75 ________
11. 31% of 148 ________
12. 53% of 539 ________

13. In 2004, about $38 out of every $100 spent on advertising was spent on television advertising. The amount spent on radio advertising was about 21% as much as was spent on television advertising. How much of every $100 spent on advertising was spent on radio advertising? ________

Use 1% or 10% to estimate the percent of each number.

14. 32% of 46 ________
15. 81% of 36 ________
16. 15% of 44 ________
17. 21% of 62 ________
18. 3% of 72 ________
19. 62% of 88 ________
20. 12% of 48 ________
21. 65% of 124 ________
22. 18% of 147 ________
23. 5% of 837 ________
24. 37% of 213 ________
25. 2% of 188 ________

26. The Fresh Acres Swim Club has a $35,000 budget for pool maintenance this year. The club members have agreed to raise the budget by 4%. Estimate the pool maintenance budget for next year. ________

Name ______________________ Date ______________ Class ______________

LESSON 6-4

Practice B

Percent of a Number

Find the percent of each number.

1. 25% of 56 ________
2. 10% of 110 ________
3. 5% of 150 ________
4. 90% of 180 ________
5. 125% of 48 ________
6. 225% of 88 ________
7. 2% of 350 ________
8. 285% of 200 ________
9. 150% of 125 ________
10. 46% of 235 ________
11. 78% of 410 ________
12. 0.5% of 64 ________

Find the percent of each number. Check whether your answer is reasonable.

13. 55% of 900 ________
14. 140% of 50 ________
15. 75% of 128 ________
16. 3% of 600 ________
17. 16% of 85 ________
18. 22% of 105 ________
19. 0.7% of 110 ________
20. 95% of 500 ________
21. 3% of 750 ________
22. 162% of 250 ________
23. 18% of 90 ________
24. 23.2% of 125 ________
25. 0.1% of 950 ________
26. 11% of 300 ________
27. 52% of 410 ________
28. 250% of 12 ________
29. The largest frog in the world is the goliath, found in West Africa. This type of frog can grow to be 12 inches long. The smallest frog in the world is about 4% as long as the goliath. What is the approximate length of the smallest frog in the world?

____

Name ______________________ Date ______________ Class ______________

LESSON 6-5

Practice B

Solving Percent Problems

1. 50 is 40% of what number?

2. 12 is 25% of what number?

3. 18 is what percent of 60?

4. 12 is what percent of 96?

5. 4% of what number is 25?

6. 80% of what number is 160?

7. What percent of 55 is 22?

8. What percent of 75 is 6?

9. 15 is 30% of what number?

10. 8% of what number is 2?

11. 7 is what percent of 105?

12. 24 is 40% of what number?

13. 10% of what number is 14?

14. 16 is what percent of 200?

15. What percent of 32 is 4?

16. What percent of 150 is 60?

17. 1% of what number is 11?

18. 20% of what number is 14?

19. The sales tax on a $750 computer at J & M Computers is $48.75. What is the sales tax rate?

20. A hardcover book sells for $24 at The Bookmart. Ben pays a total of $25.02 for the book. What is the sales tax rate?

Name ______________________ Date ______________ Class ______________

LESSON 6-6

Practice B

Percent of Change

Find each percent of change. Round answers to the nearest tenth, if necessary.

1. 20 is decreased to 11 ____________
2. 24 is increased to 30 ____________
3. 56 is decreased to 14 ____________
4. 25 is increased to 100 ____________
5. 18 is increased to 45 ____________
6. 90 is decreased to 75 ____________
7. 126 is decreased to 48 ____________
8. 65 is increased to 144 ____________
9. 42 is increased to 72 ____________
10. 84 is decreased to 8 ____________
11. 95 is increased to 145 ____________
12. 248 is decreased to 200 ____________
13. 105 is decreased to 32 ____________
14. 75 is increased to 350 ____________
15. 93 is decreased to 90 ____________
16. 16 is decreased to 2 ____________
17. A backpack that normally sells for $39 is on sale for 33% off. Find the amount of the discount and the sale price.

____

18. A sporting goods store is having a closeout on a certain style of running shoes. They are marked 55% off the regular price. The regular price is $79.95. Find the amount of the discount and the sale price.

____

19. A gallery owner purchased a very old painting for $3,000. The painting sells at a 325% increase in price. What is the retail price of the painting?

____

20. In August, the Simons' water bill was $48. In September, it was 15% lower. What was the Simons' water bill in September?

____

Name ______________________ Date ______________ Class ______________

LESSON 6-7

Practice B

Simple Interest

Find each missing value.

1. $p = \$1,500$, $r = 5\%$, $t = 3$ years

   $I =$ ____________

2. $p = \$6,000$, $r = 4\%$, $t = 2$ years

   $I =$ ____________

3. $I = \$30$, $r = 4\%$, $t = 2$ years

   $p =$ ____________

4. $I = \$180$, $r = 5\%$, $t = 3$ years

   $p =$ ____________

5. $I = \$20$, $p = \$250$, $t = 2$ years

   $r =$ ____________

6. $I = \$144$, $p = \$800$, $t = 3$ years

   $r =$ ____________

7. $p = \$525$, $r = 3\%$, $t = 1$ year

   $I =$ ____________

8. $p = \$3,200$, $r = 6\%$, $t = 4$ years

   $I =$ ____________

9. $I = \$450$, $r = 6\%$, $t = 4$ years

   $p =$ ____________

10. $I = \$1,440$, $r = 3\%$, $t = 5$ years

    $p =$ ____________

11. $I = \$1,275$, $p = \$5,100$, $t = 5$ years

    $r =$ ____________

12. $I = \$3,920$, $p = \$14,000$, $t = 4$ years

    $r =$ ____________

13. $p = \$1,300$, $r = 4.5\%$, $t = 6$ months

    $I =$ ____________

14. $I = \$47.25$, $r = 3.5\%$, $t = 1.5$ years

    $p =$ ____________

15. $I = \$891$, $p = \$2,700$, $t = 5.5$ years

    $r =$ ____________

16. $I = \$126$, $p = \$400$, $t = 9$ years

    $r =$ ____________

17. You deposit \$2,500 in an account that earns 4% simple interest. How long will it be before the total amount is \$3,000? ____________

18. You deposit \$5,000 in account that earns 6.5% simple interest. How much will be in the account after 3 years? ____________

19. A deposit of \$10,000 was made to an account the year you were born. After 12 years, the account is worth \$16,600. What simple interest rate did the account earn? ____________

20. How long will it take for \$6,500 to double at a simple interest rate of 7%? Round to the nearest tenth of a year. ____________

Name ______________________ Date ____________ Class ____________

LESSON 7-1

Practice B

Frequency Tables, Stem-and-Leaf Plots, and Line Plots

The table shows the heights of students in Ms. Blaire's class. Use the table for Exercises 1 and 2.

	Height (in.)
Males	60, 45, 48, 57, 62, 59, 57, 60, 56, 58, 61, 52, 55
Females	49, 52, 56, 48, 51, 60, 47, 53, 55, 58, 54

1. Make a cumulative frequency table of the data.

Heights of Students

Height (in.)	Frequency	Cumulative Frequency

2. How many of the students were less than 60 in tall? ____________

3. Make a stem-and-leaf plot of the data.

Heights of Students

Stem	Leaves

Key:

4. How many of the students were less than 50 inches tall? ____________

5. Make a line plot of the data.

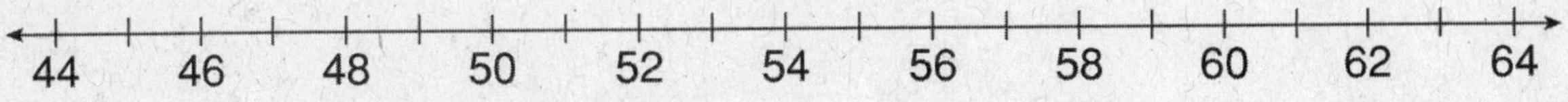

6. Which height occurred the greatest number of times? ____________

Name ______________________ Date ______________ Class ______________

LESSON 7-2

Practice B

Mean, Median, Mode, and Range

Find the mean, median, mode, and range of each data set.

1. 46, 35, 23, 37, 29, 53, 43

____

2. 72, 56, 47, 69, 75, 48, 56, 57

____

3. 19, 11, 80, 19, 27, 19, 10, 25, 15

____

4. 7, 8, 20, 6, 9, 11, 10, 8, 9, 8

____

5. The line plot shows the number of hours 15 students said they spent on homework in one week. Which measure of central tendency best describes the data? Justify your answer.

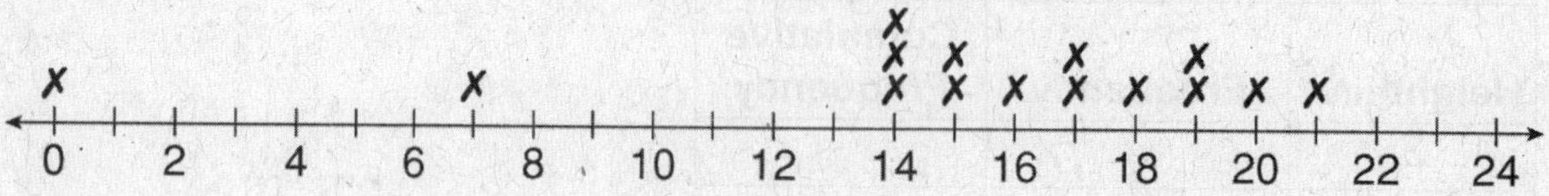

____

____

Identify the outlier in each data set. Then determine how the outlier affects the mean, median, and mode of the data. Then tell which measure of central tendency best describes the data with and without the outlier.

6. 14, 16, 13, 15, 5, 16, 12

____

7. 48, 46, 52, 92, 57, 58, 52, 61, 56

____

____

____

Name ______________________ Date ______________ Class ______________

LESSON 7-3

Practice B

Bar Graphs and Histograms

The bar graph shows the elevations of the highest points in several states. Use the graph for Exercises 1–3.

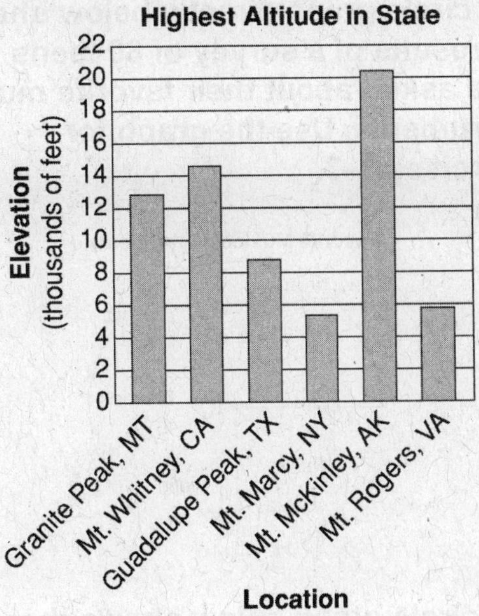

1. Which state has the highest elevation?

   ____

2. About how much higher is Granite Peak than Guadalupe Peak?

   ____

3. About how much higher is Mount Whitney than Mount Marcy?

   ____

4. The table shows the approximate mean length and width of three states. Make a double-bar graph of the data.

State	Length (mi)	Width (mi)
Florida	500	160
New York	330	283
Virginia	430	200

Key: ______________

5. The list shows the bowling scores of the first game played by a group of bowlers on Thursday night. Make a histogram of the data.
   96, 110, 132, 128, 105, 94, 116, 95, 126, 114, 123, 136, 121, 99

Name ______________________ Date ______________ Class ______________

LESSON 7-4

Practice B

Reading and Interpreting Circle Graphs

The circle graph directly below shows the results of a survey of 80 teens who were asked about their favorite musical instruments. Use the graph for Exercises 1–3.

Favorite Musical Instruments

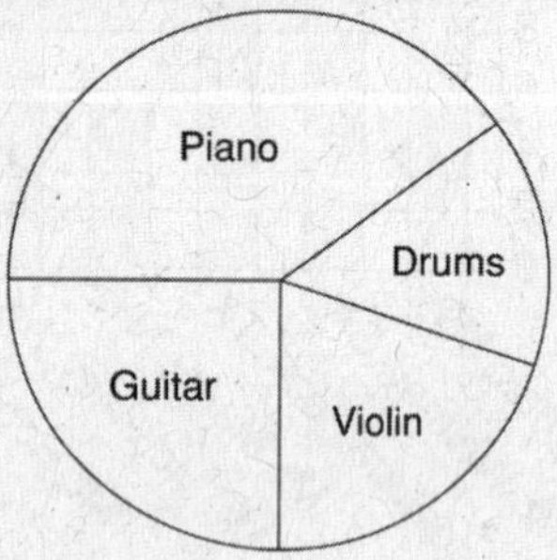

1. Did more teens pick piano or drums?

2. About what percent of teens picked guitar?

3. According to the survey, 20% of teens chose violin. How many teens chose violin?

The circle graph below shows the results of a survey of 100 people who were asked about their favorite vacation destinations. Use the graph for Exercises 4–6.

Favorite Vacation Destinations

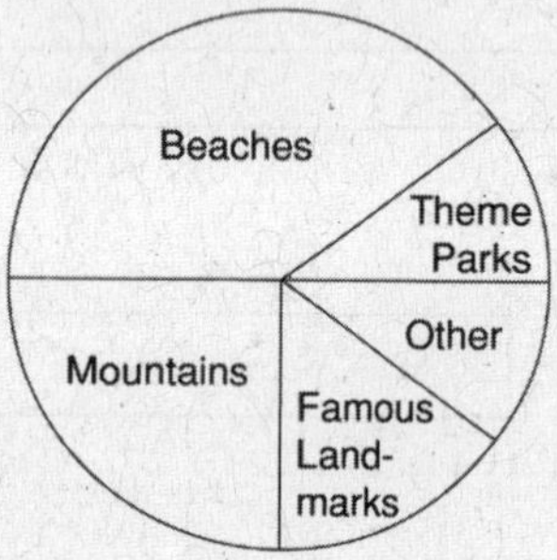

4. Did more people pick mountains or beaches?

5. About what percent of people picked mountains?

6. According to the survey, 15% of the people chose famous landmarks. How many people chose famous landmarks?

Decide whether a bar graph or a circle graph would best display the information. Explain your answer.

7. number of tornadoes in each state during one year

8. the number of pounds of Macintosh apples sold compared with the total number of pounds of apples sold at a market in one day

Name ______________________ Date ______________ Class ______________

LESSON 7-5

Practice B

Box-and-Whisker Plots

1. Use the data to make a box-and-whisker plot.
19, 46, 37, 16, 24, 47, 23, 19, 31, 25, 42

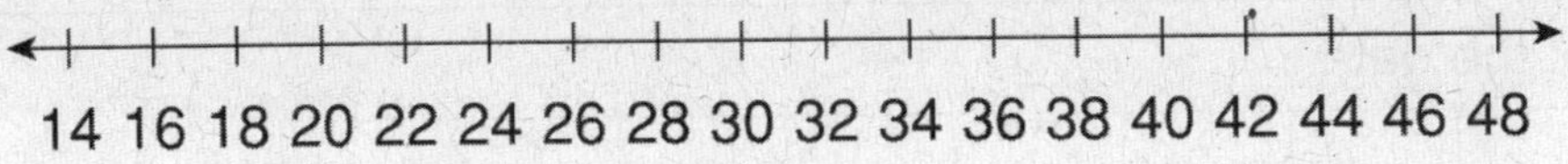

Use the box-and-whisker plot of games won per season by the New York Yankees and the Arizona Diamondbacks for 1998–2005 for Exercises 2–4.

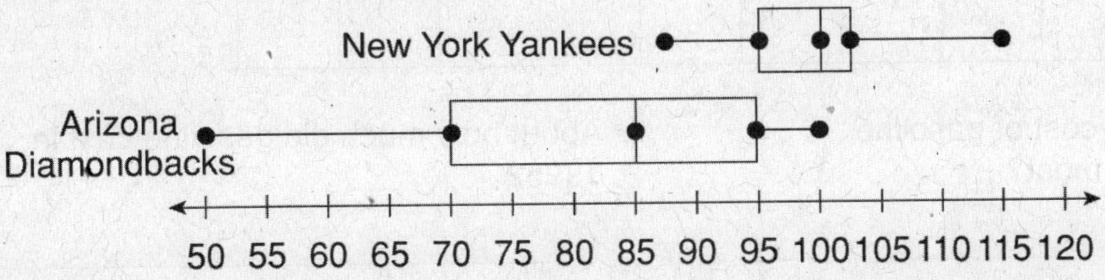

2. Which team has the greater median number of games won? ______________

3. Which team has the greater interquartile range of games won? ______________

4. Which team appears to have a more predictable performance? ______________

Use the box-and-whisker plot of nightly tip totals that a waitress gets at two different restaurants for Exercises 5–7.

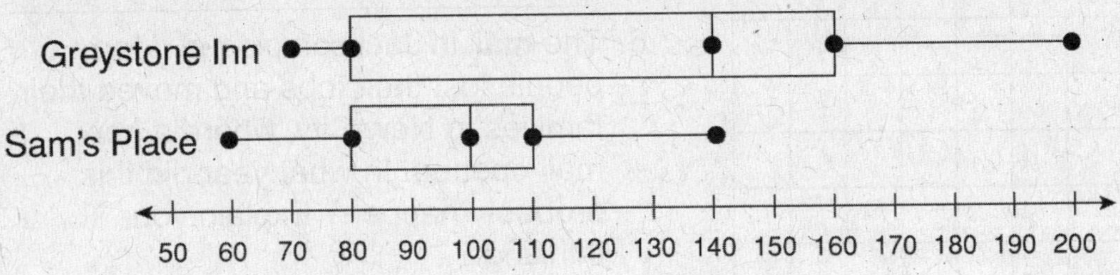

5. At which restaurant is the median tip total greater? ______________

6. At which restaurant is the interquartile range of tip totals greater?

____

7. At which restaurant does the tip total appear to be more predictable?

____

Name ______________________ Date ____________ Class ____________

LESSON 7-6

Practice B

Line Graphs

Use the table for Exercises 1–3.

Retail Price of Regular Gasoline in the United States (to the nearest cent)

Year	1990	1992	1994	1996	1998	2000	2002	2004
Price Per Gallon	\$1.16	\$1.13	\$1.11	\$1.23	\$1.06	\$1.54	\$1.32	\$1.82

1. Make a line graph of the data.

2. When did the cost of gasoline decrease the most?

____

3. About how much did gasoline cost in 1995?

____

The table below shows the student population at elementary schools in two cities, New City and Jackson.

Year	1996	1997	1998	1999	2000	2001	2002	2003
New City	450	460	440	430	495	500	600	645
Jackson	500	475	450	525	430	440	485	480

4. Make a double-line graph of the data.

Key:

5. During which year did New City's school population increase the most?

____

6. The mall in Jackson closed. Many people lost their jobs and moved their families to New City, where a new mall opened. In what year did this probably happen? Explain your thinking.

____

____

____

Name ______________________ Date ______________ Class ______________

LESSON 7-7

Practice B

Choosing an Appropriate Display

Choose the type of graph that would best represent this data.

1. the number of points scored by five different basketball players in a game

____

2. the distribution of test scores in a math class

____

3. the students who are in the chess club, the debating club, and the computer club, and the students who are in more than one of those clubs

____

4. the percent of total income a family uses for rent, food, clothing, entertainment, savings and other expenditures

____

The table shows the earnings of The Sandman Company during each of five years. Explain why each display does or does not appropriately represent the data.

Year	Earnings (millions of dollars)
2001	1
2002	3
2003	8
2004	12
2005	16

5.

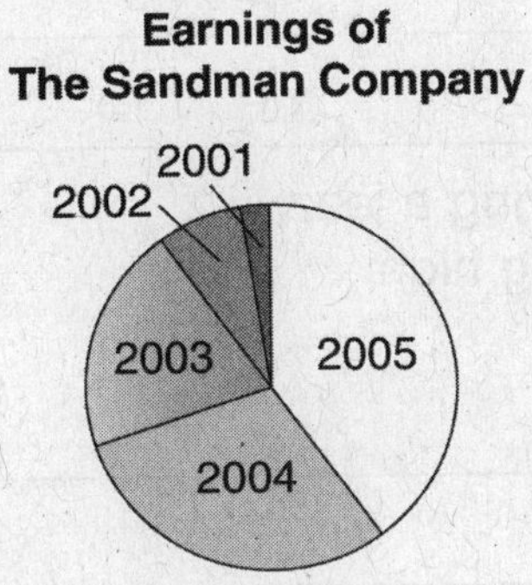

____

6.

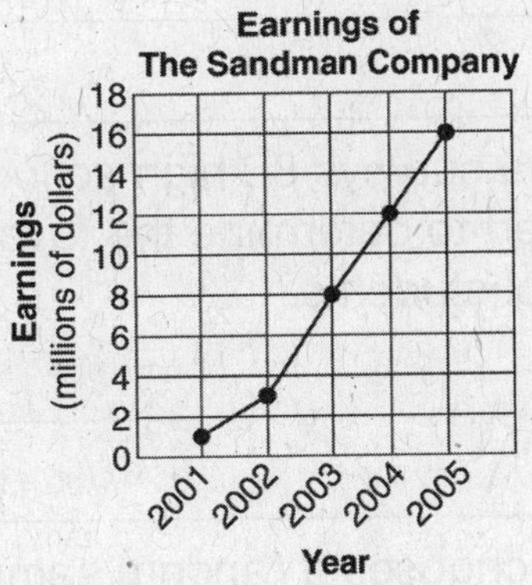

____

Name ______________________ Date ______________ Class ______________

LESSON 7-8

Practice B

Populations and Samples

1. Determine which sampling method will better represent the entire population. Justify your answer.

Reading Habits of High School Students	
Sampling Method	**Results of Survey**
Dinah surveys 48 students who she knows.	91% have read a novel in the past month.
Suki gives survey forms to 100 students who were randomly chosen from a school attendance list.	59% have read a novel in the past month.

____

____

____

For Problems 2 and 3, determine whether each sample may be biased. Explain.

2. An on-line bookseller randomly chooses 200 book buyers from its database and then surveys those book buyers to find out if they were satisfied with the time it took to deliver their orders.

____

____

3. Milena surveys 80 high school students who are leaving a jazz concert to determine the favorite type of music among high school students.

____

____

4. Zack chooses a random sample of 50 out of 400 students. He finds that 7 of them have traveled to a foreign country. Zack claims that over 50 of the 400 students have traveled to a foreign country. Do you agree? Explain your answer.

____

5. A mint produces 150,000 souvenir coins each year. In a random sample of 400 coins, 3 have a misprint. Predict the number of coins that will have misprints in a year.

Name ______________________ Date ______________ Class ______________

LESSON 7-9

Practice B

Scatter Plots

The table shows boys' average heights in inches from ages 6 through 13. Use the table for Exercises 1–3.

Age	6	7	8	9	10	11	12	13
Height (in.)	$46\frac{3}{4}$	49	51	$53\frac{1}{4}$	$55\frac{1}{4}$	$57\frac{1}{4}$	59	61

1. Make a scatter plot of the data.

2. Describe the relationship between the data sets.

____

____

3. What kind of correlation does the plot show?

____

Write *positive, negative,* or *no correlation* to describe each relationship.

4.

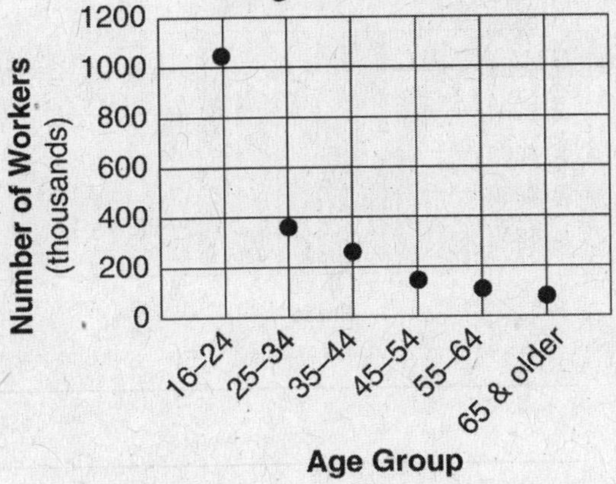

____

5.

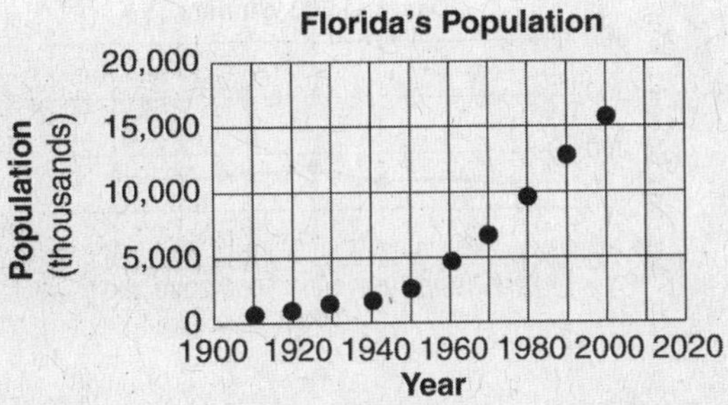

____

6. student test scores and the number of students who walk to school

____

7. the grade levels of students and their ages in months

____

8. the year a state entered the union and the number of years as a state

____

9. ages of students and their grades on tests

____

Name ______________________ Date ______________ Class ______________

LESSON 7-10

Practice B

Misleading Graphs

1. Which graph could be misleading? Why?

Graph A

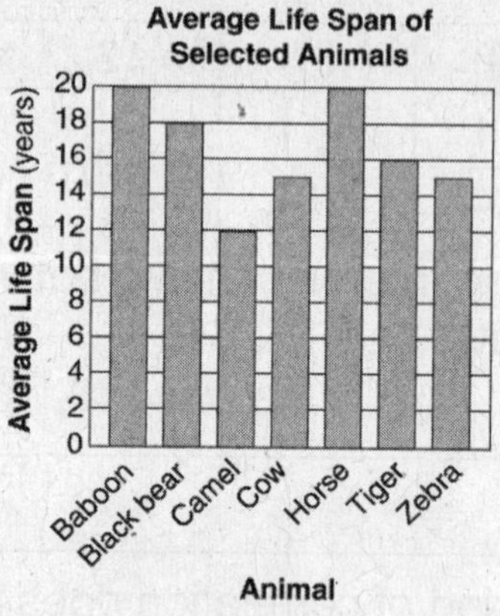

Graph B

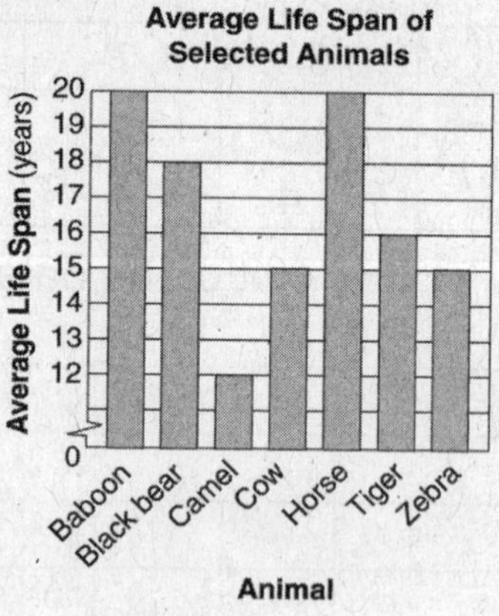

____

____

Explain why each graph could be misleading.

2.

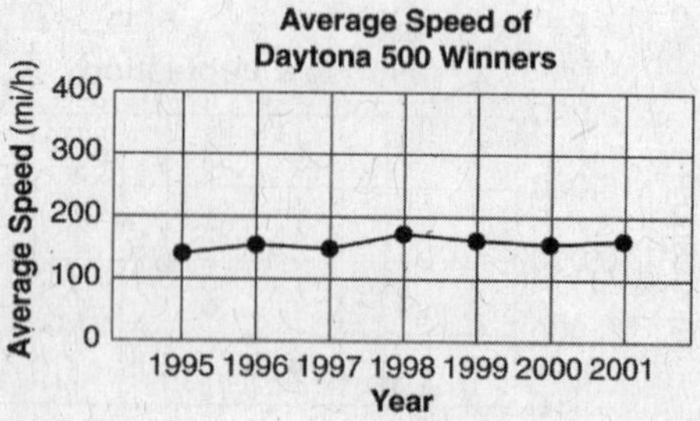

____

____

____

3.

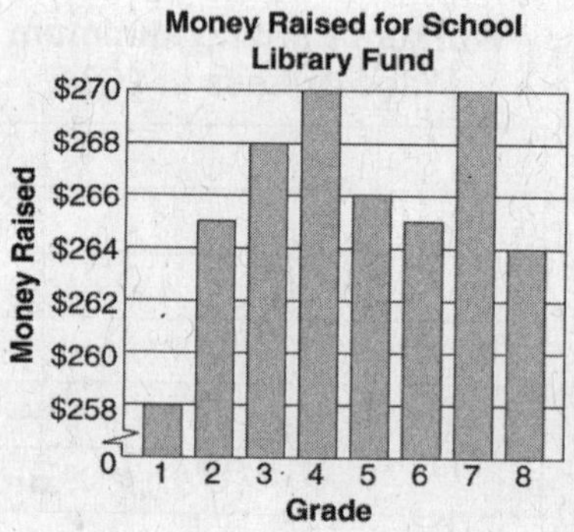

____

____

____

Name ______________________ Date ______________ Class ______________

LESSON 8-1

Practice B

Building Blocks of Geometry

Identify the figures in the diagram.

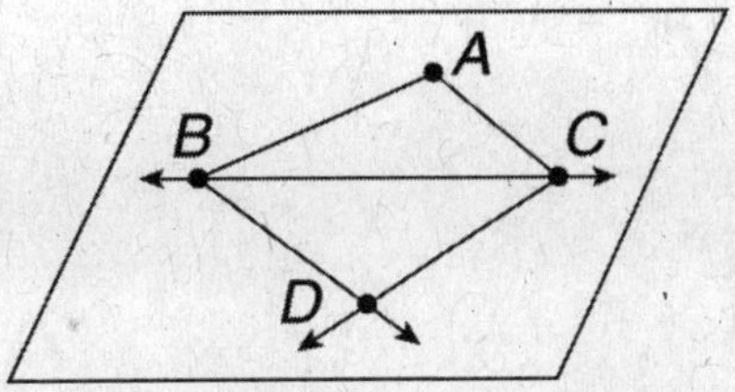

1. three points ______________________
2. one line ______________________
3. a plane ______________________
4. four rays ______________________
5. three line segments ______________________

Identify the figures in the diagram.

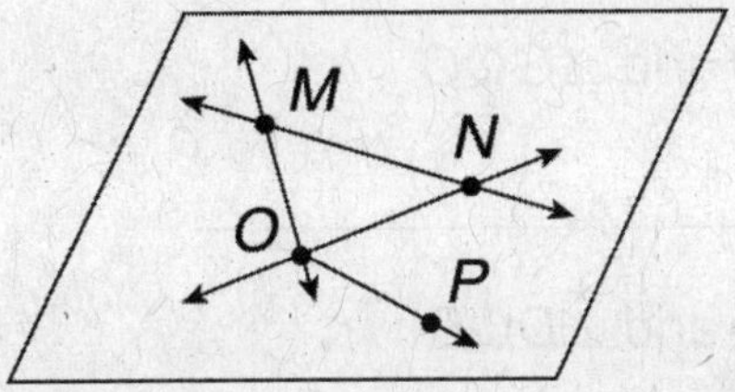

6. four points ______________________
7. three lines ______________________
8. a plane ______________________
9. three rays ______________________
10. four line segments ______________________

Identify the figures in the diagram.

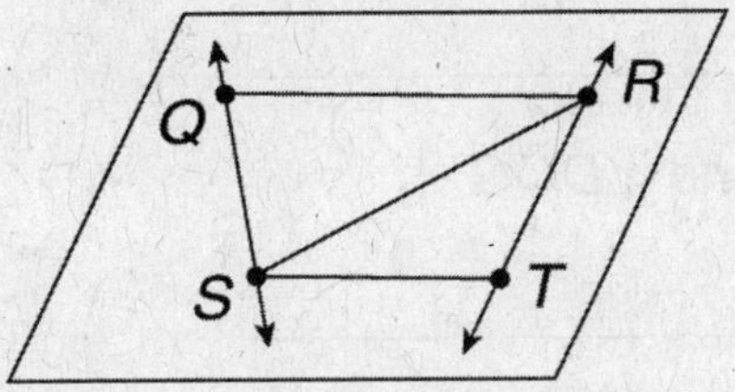

11. four points ______________________
12. two lines ______________________
13. a plane ______________________
14. four rays ______________________
15. five line segments ______________________

16. Identify the line segments that are congruent in the figure.

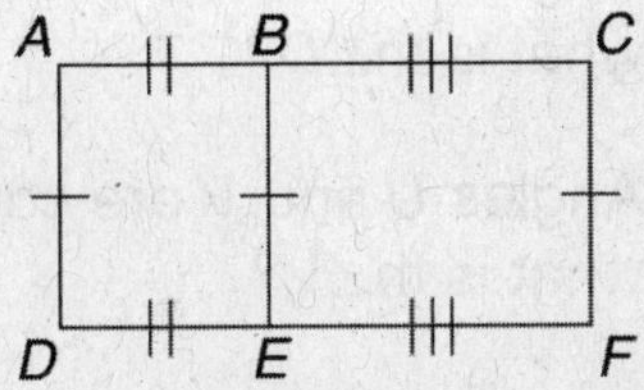

____

____

Name ______________________ Date ______________ Class ______________

LESSON 8-2

Practice B
Classifying Angles

Tell whether each angle is acute, right, obtuse, or straight.

1. 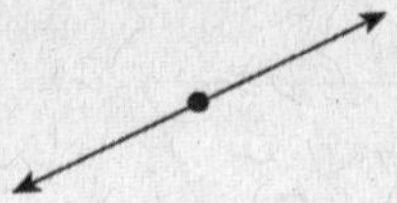

____

2. 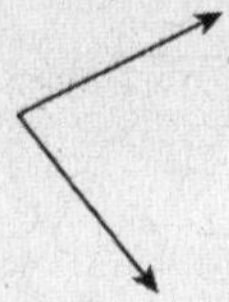

____

3. 

____

Use the diagram to tell whether the angles are complementary, supplementary or neither.

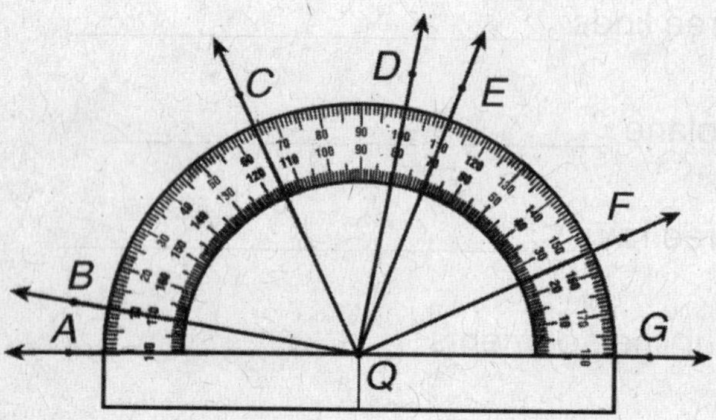

4. ∠*AQC* and ∠*GQC*

____

5. ∠*BQD* and ∠*DQE*

____

6. ∠*CQE* and ∠*EQF*

____

7. ∠*GQF* and ∠*FQE*

____

8. ∠*BQC* and ∠*DQC*

____

9. Angles *W* and *X* are supplementary. If m∠*W* is 37°, what is m∠*X*? ______________

10. Angles *S* and *T* are complementary. If m∠*S* is 64°, what is m∠*T*? ______________

11. Angles *C* and *D* are supplementary. If m∠*C* is 83°, what is m∠*D*? ______________

12. Angles *U* and *V* are complementary. If m∠*U* is 41°, what is m∠*V*? ______________

Name ______________________ Date ______________ Class ______________

LESSON 8-3

Practice B

Line and Angle Relationships

Tell whether the lines appear parallel, perpendicular, or skew.

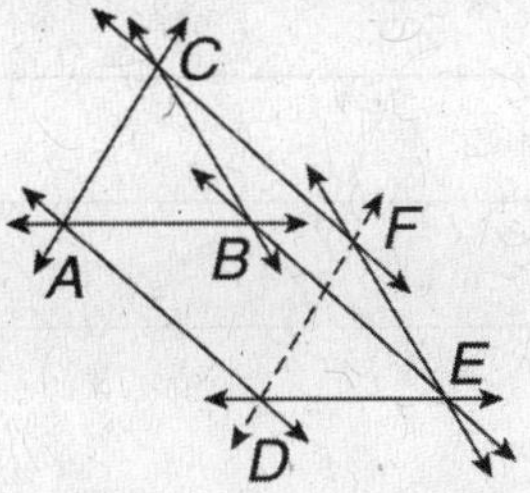

1. $\overleftrightarrow{AB}$ and $\overleftrightarrow{DE}$ ______________

2. $\overleftrightarrow{EF}$ and $\overleftrightarrow{CF}$ ______________

3. $\overleftrightarrow{AB}$ and $\overleftrightarrow{AD}$ ______________

4. $\overleftrightarrow{BC}$ and $\overleftrightarrow{DE}$ ______________

Tell whether the lines appear parallel, perpendicular, or skew.

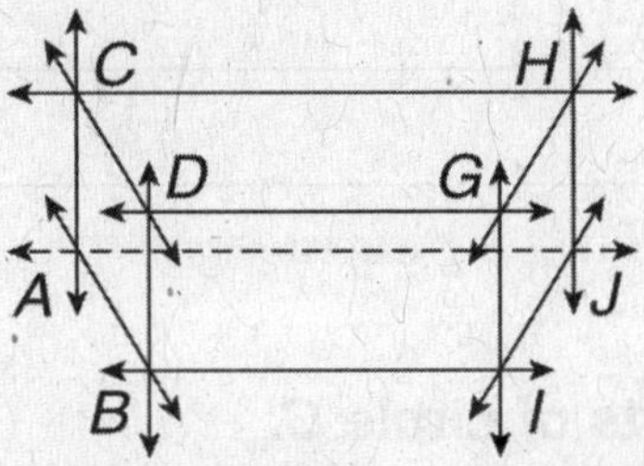

5. $\overleftrightarrow{BD}$ and $\overleftrightarrow{DG}$ ______________

6. $\overleftrightarrow{AB}$ and $\overleftrightarrow{BD}$ ______________

7. $\overleftrightarrow{DG}$ and $\overleftrightarrow{IJ}$ ______________

8. $\overleftrightarrow{AB}$ and $\overleftrightarrow{CD}$ ______________

Line *x* || line *y*. Find the measure of each angle.

9. ∠1 and ∠6

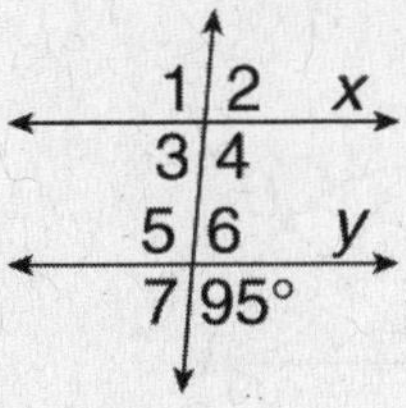

____

10. ∠4 and ∠8

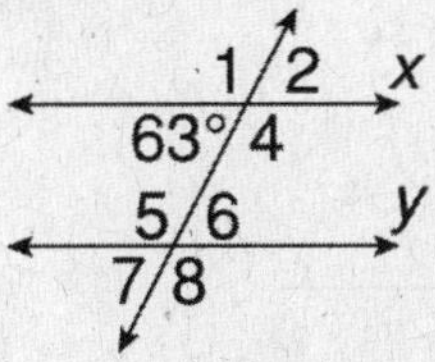

____

11. ∠4 and ∠6

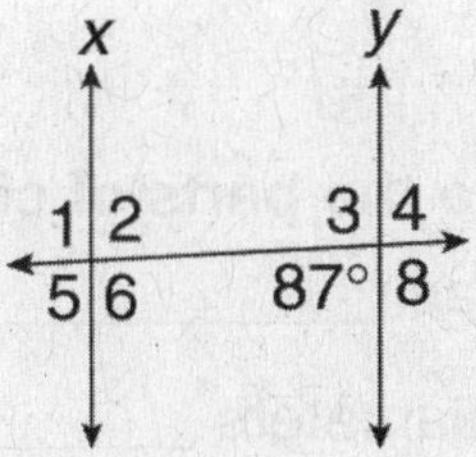

____

12. ∠2 and ∠4

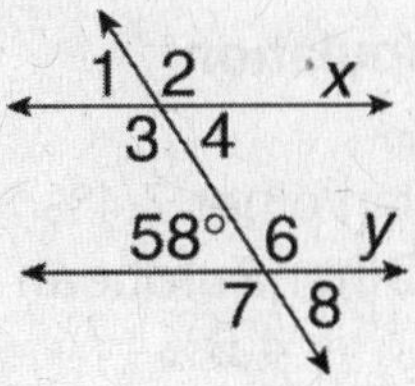

____

13. ∠5 and ∠7

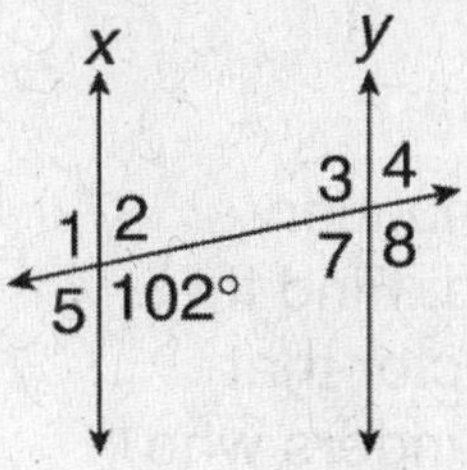

____

14. ∠7 and ∠8

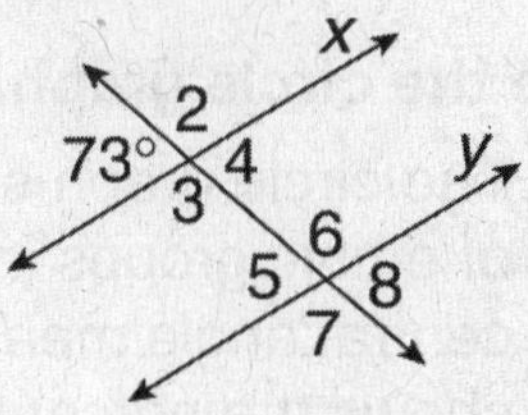

____

Name ______________________ Date ______________ Class ______________

LESSON 8-4

Practice B

Properties of Circles

Name the parts of circle *A*.

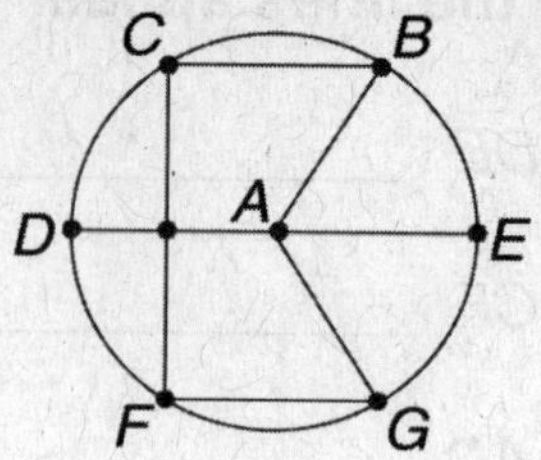

1. radii ______________________

2. diameters ______________________

3. chords ______________________

Name the parts of circle *H*.

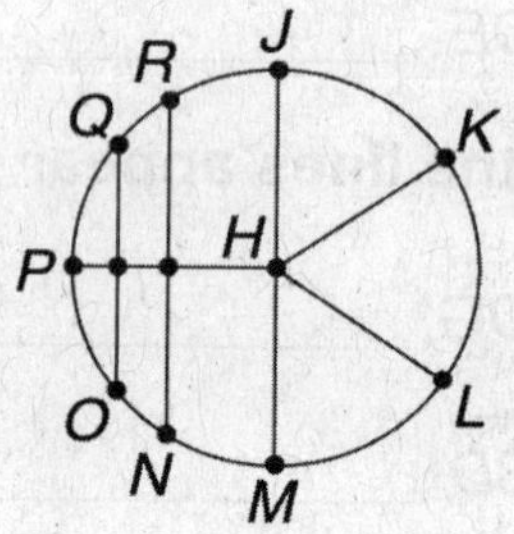

4. radii ______________________

5. diameters ______________________

6. chords ______________________

Name the parts of circle *C*.

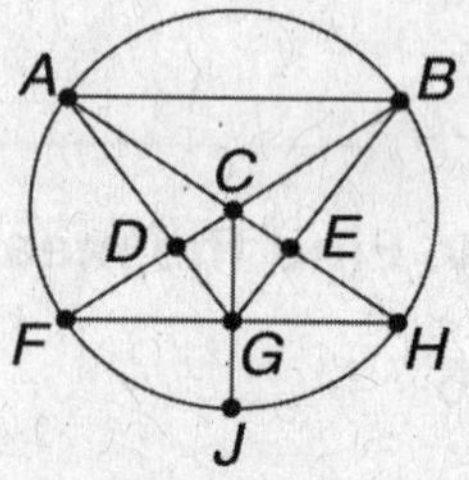

7. radii ______________________

8. diameters ______________________

9. chords ______________________

Name the parts of circle *Z*.

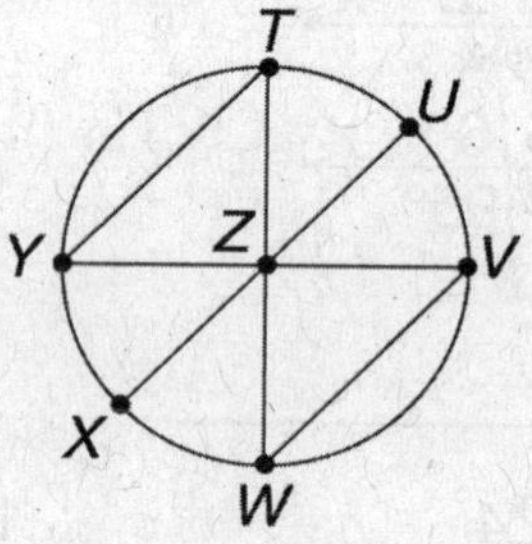

10. radii ______________________

11. diameters ______________________

12. chords ______________________

Use the circle graph.

13. The circle graph shows the distribution of ethnic groups in New Zealand. Find the central angle measure of the sector that shows the percent of New Zealanders who are Maori.

____

New Zealand Population

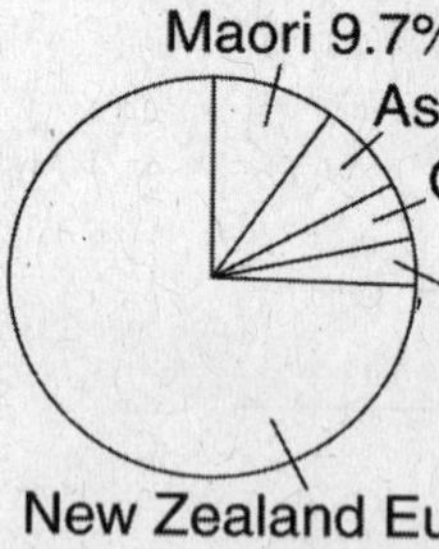

Name ______________________ Date ______________ Class ______________

LESSON 8-5

Practice B

Classifying Polygons

Determine whether each figure is a polygon. If it is not, explain why not.

1.

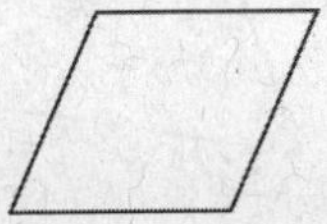

2.

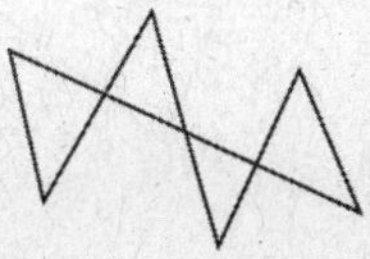

3.

4.

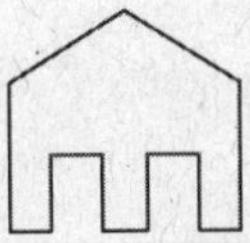

5.

6.

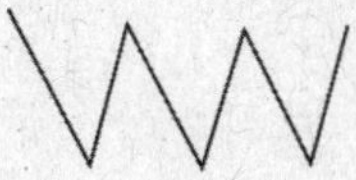

Name each polygon.

7.

8.

9.

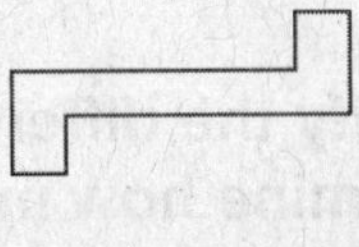

10.

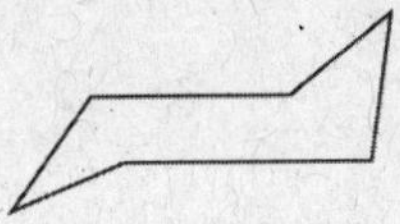

11.

12.

Name each figure and tell whether it is a regular polygon. If it is not, explain why not.

13.

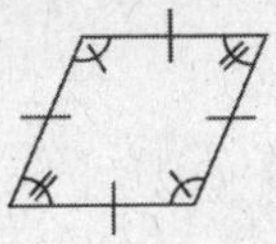

14.

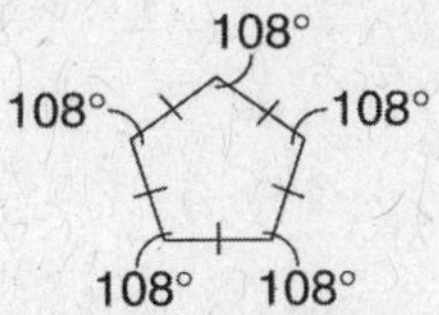

15.

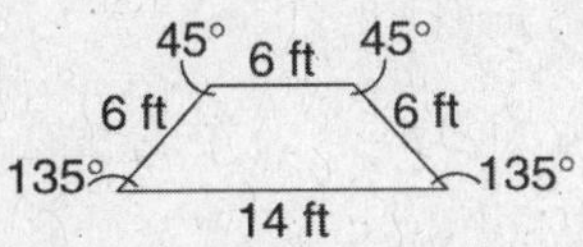

Name ______________________ Date ______________ Class ______________

LESSON 8-6

Practice B

Classifying Triangles

Classify each triangle according to its sides and angles.

1.
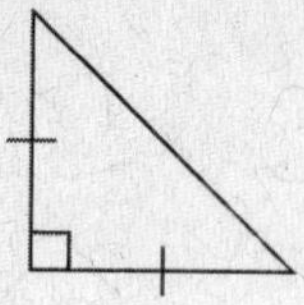

2.
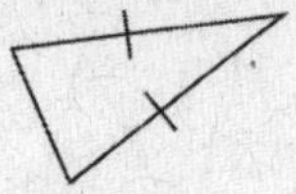

3.
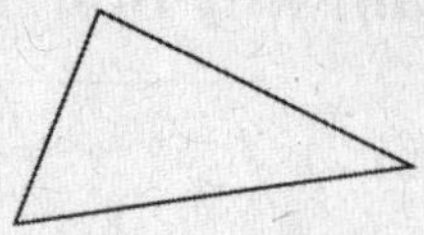

4.
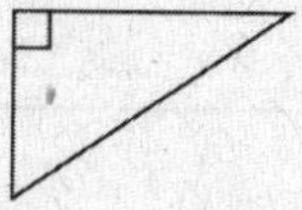

5.
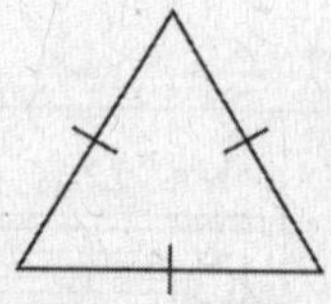

6.
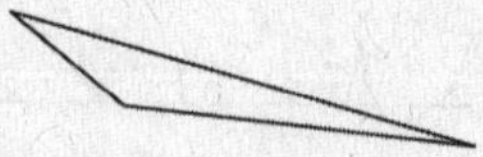

7.

8.
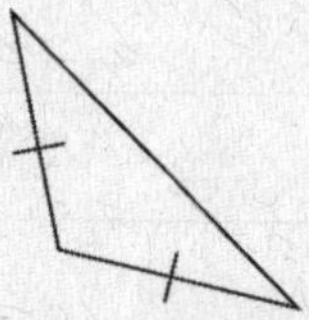

9.
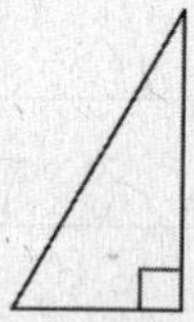

Identify the different types of triangles in each figure and determine how many of each there are.

10.
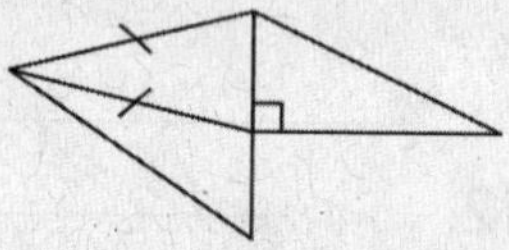

11.
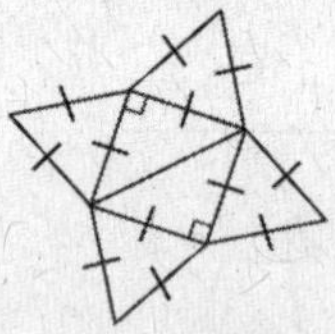

Name ______________________ Date ______________ Class ______________

LESSON 8-7

Practice B

Classifying Quadrilaterals

Give all of the names that apply to each quadrilateral. Then give the name that best describes it.

1. 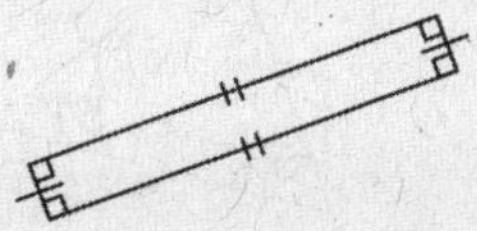

2. 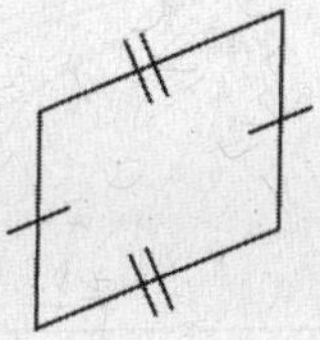

3. 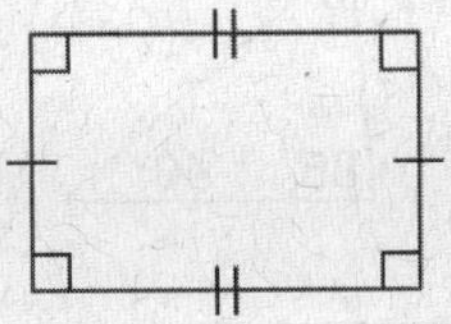

4. 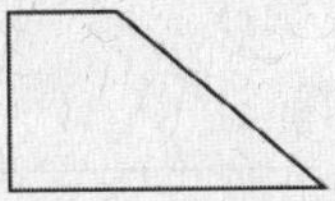

5. 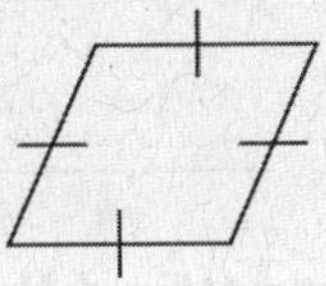

6. 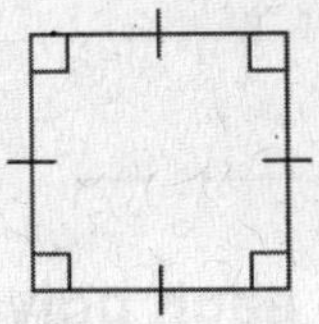

Draw each figure. If it is not possible to draw, explain why.

7. A rectangle that is not a parallelogram.

8. A rectangle that is not a square.

Name ________________________ Date ______________ Class ______________

LESSON 8-8

Practice B

Angles in Polygons

Find the unknown angle measure in each polygon.

1.

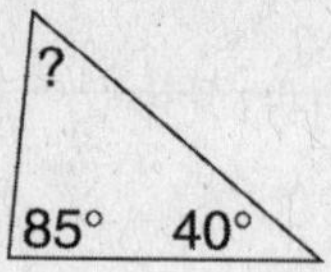

____

2.

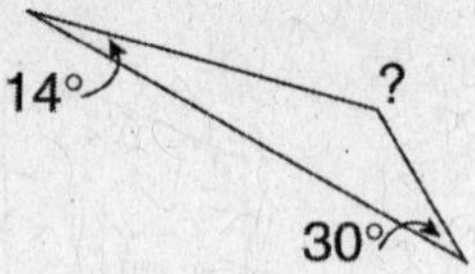

____

3.

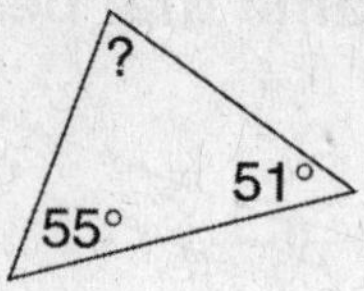

____

4.

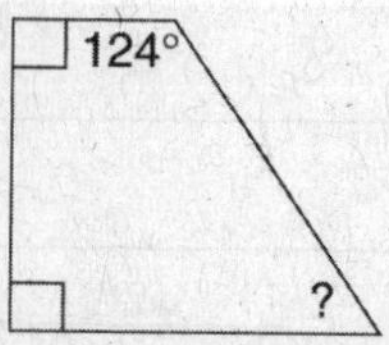

____

5.

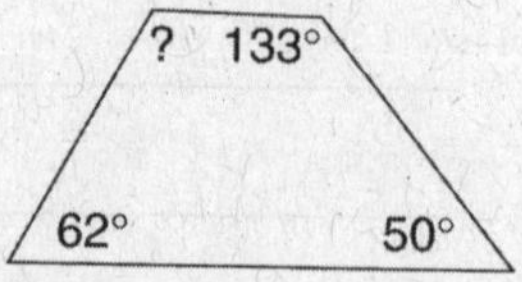

____

6.

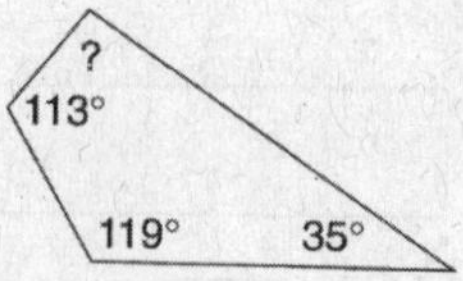

____

Divide each polygon into triangles to find the sum of its interior angles.

7.

____

8.

____

9.

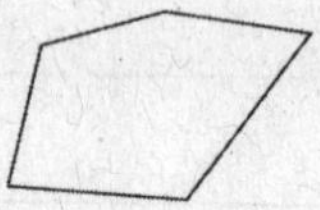

____

10.

____

11.

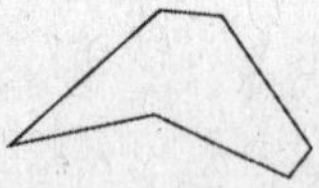

____

12.

____

13. A stop sign has the shape of a regular octagon. What is the sum of the interior angles of a stop sign?

____

Name ____________________ Date ______________ Class ______________

LESSON 8-9

Practice B

Congruent Figures

Identify any congruent figures.

1.

____

2.

____

Determine whether the triangles are congruent.

3.

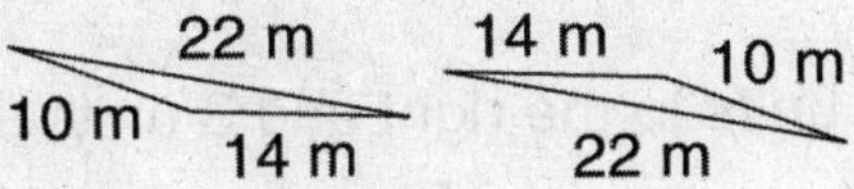

____

4.

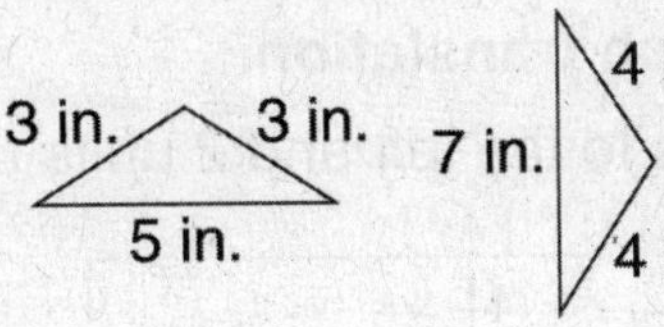

____

5.

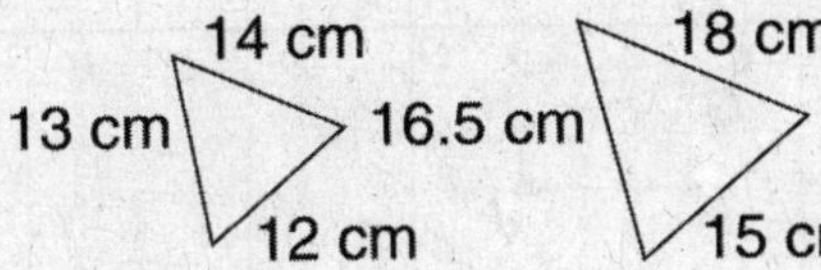

____

6.

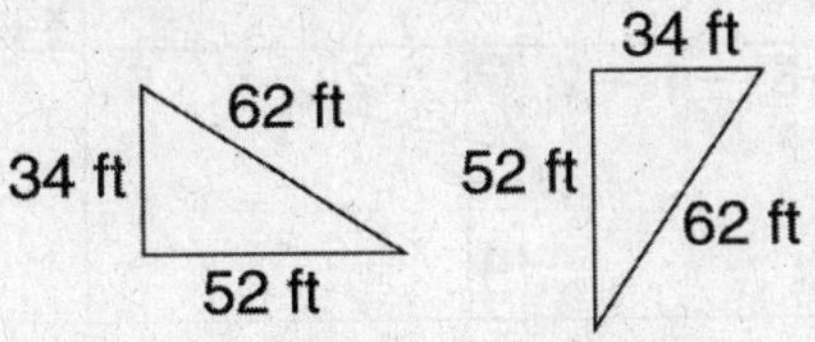

____

Determine the unknown measure or measures in each set of congruent polygons.

7.

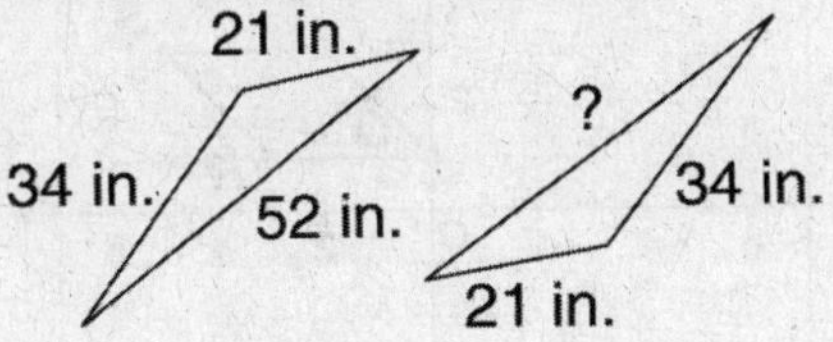

____

8.

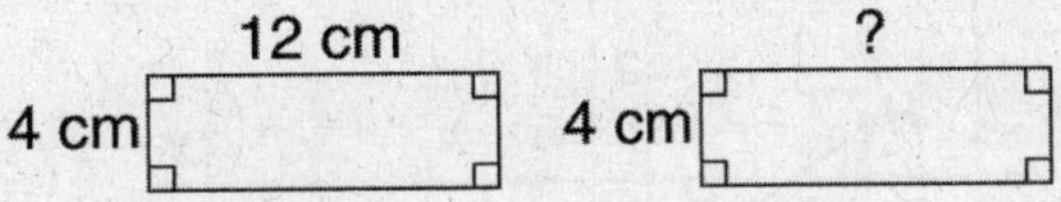

____

9.

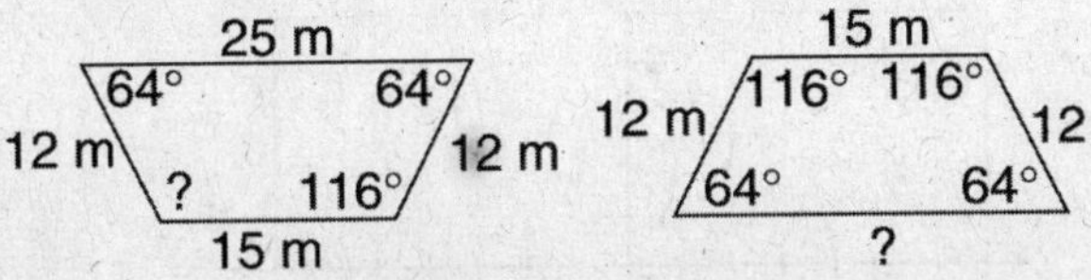

____

10.

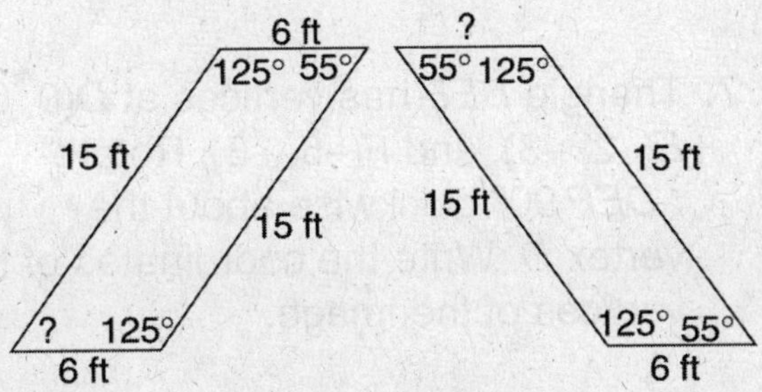

____

Name ______________________ Date ______________ Class ______________

LESSON 8-10

Practice B

Translations, Reflections, and Rotations

Identify each type of transformation.

1.

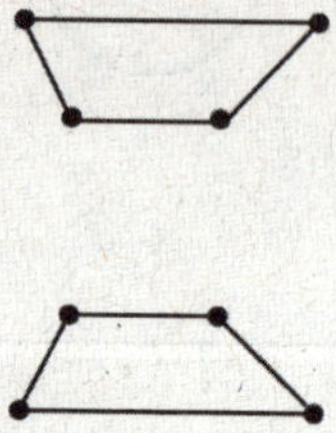

2.

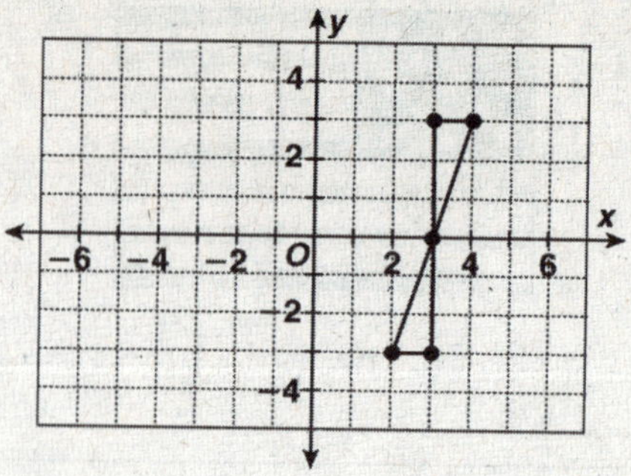

______________________ ______________________

Graph each translation.

3. 5 units to the left and 2 units up

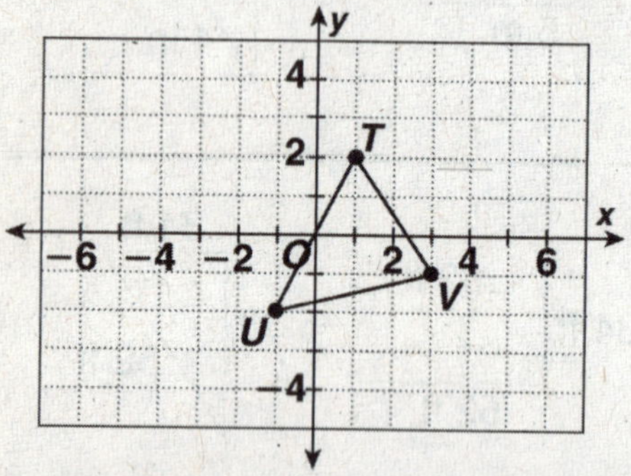

4. 4 units to the right and 3 units up

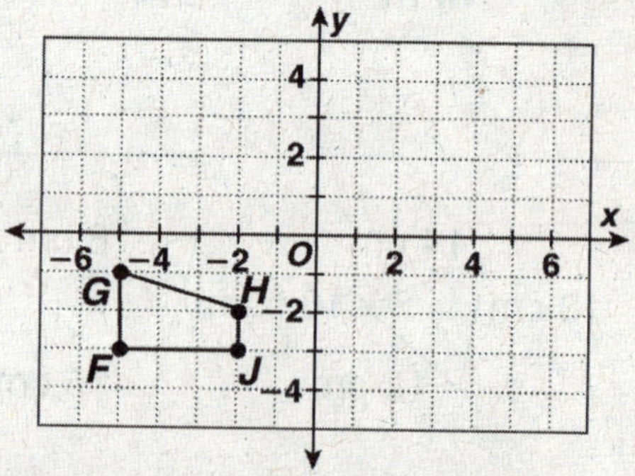

Graph the reflection of each figure across the indicated axis. Write the coordinates of the vertices of each image.

5. *x*-axis

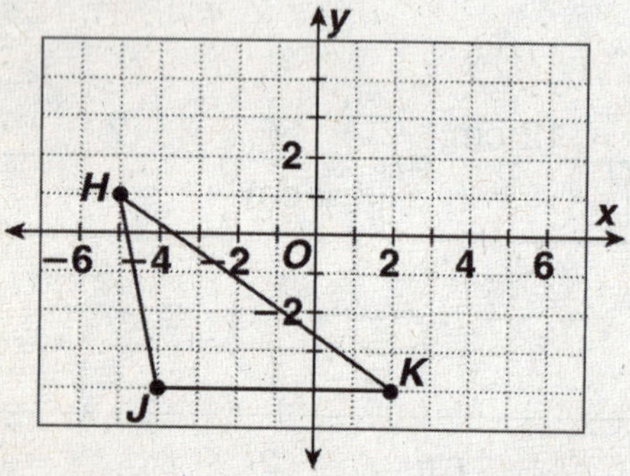

6. *y*-axis

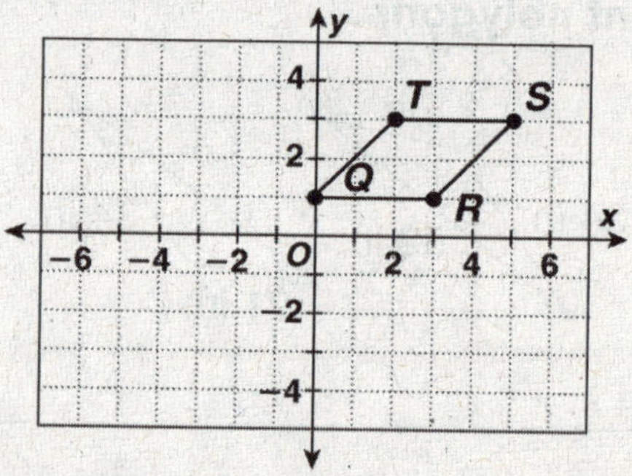

7. Triangle *DEF* has vertices at *D*(0, 0), *E*(–2, –3), and *F*(–5, –3). Rotate ΔDEF 90° clockwise about the vertex *D*. Write the coordinates of the vertices of the image.

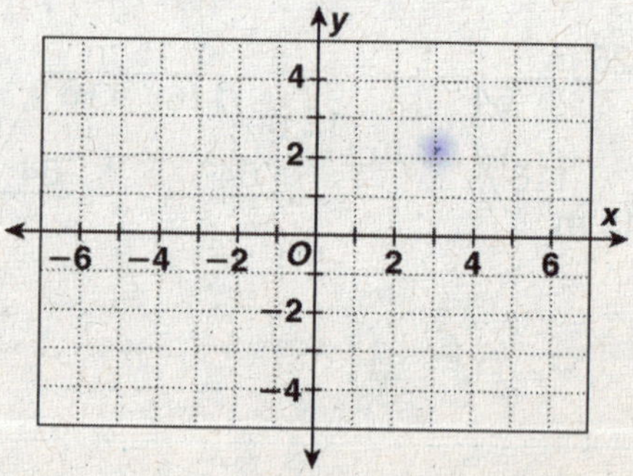

Name ______________________ Date ______________ Class ______________

LESSON 8-11

Practice B

Symmetry

Decide whether each figure has line symmetry. If it does, draw all the lines of symmetry.

1.

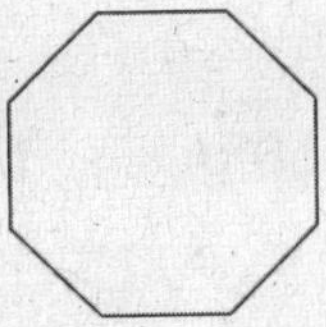

2.

3.

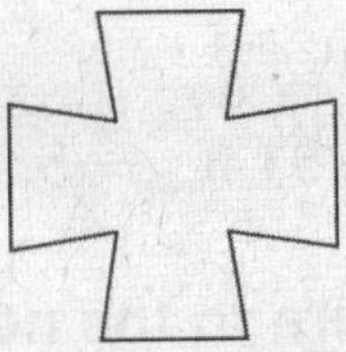

Find and draw all the lines of symmetry in each flag.

4. Iceland

5. Nauru

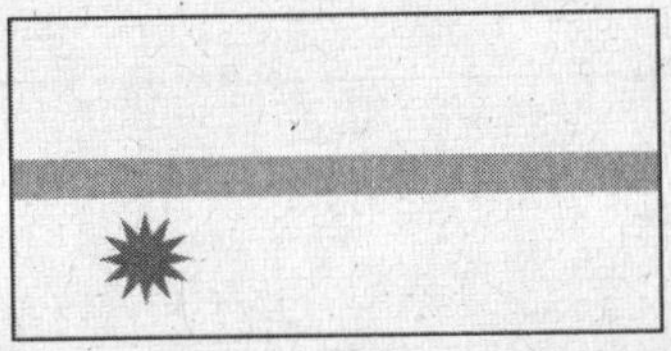

6. Burundi

Tell how many times each figure will show rotational symmetry within one full rotation.

7.

____

8.

____

9.

____

10.

____

11.

____

12.

____

Name ______________________ Date ______________ Class ______________

LESSON 9-1

Practice B

Accuracy and Precision

Circle the more precise measurement in each pair.

1. 122 km 1,230 m
2. 91.1 kg 91 kg
3. 14 cm 14 mm
4. 5,281 ft 5,281 in.
5. 1 mi 1,000.3 mi
6. 550 g 5 kg

Measure to the nearest half, fourth, and eighth inch. Which measurement is the most accurate?

7. 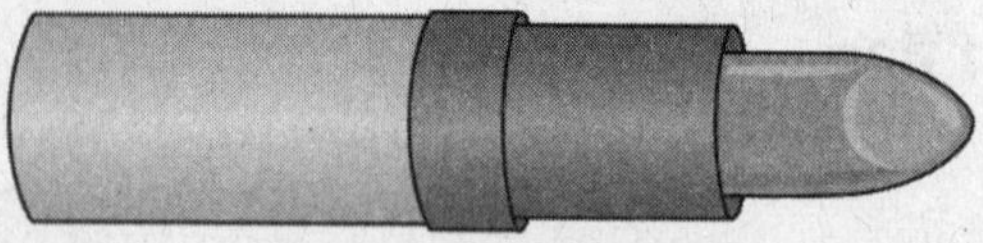

____

8. 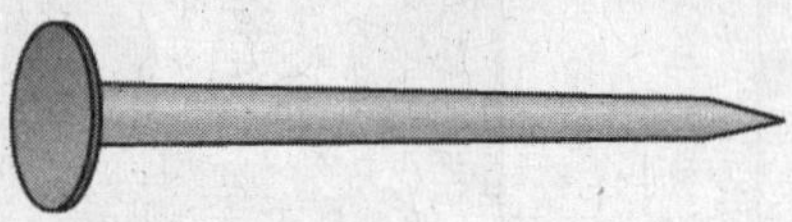

____

Estimate each measurement.

9. 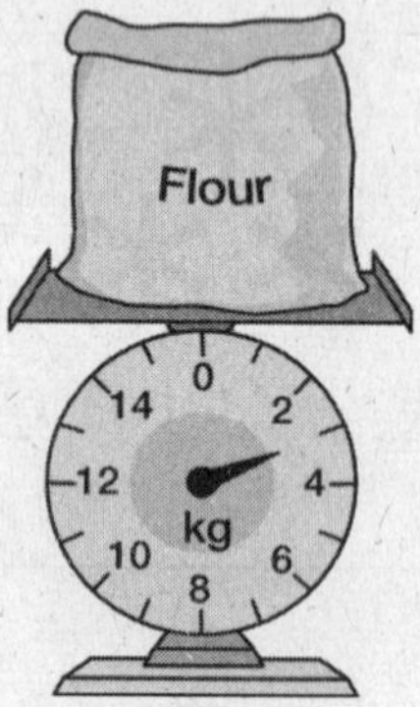

____

10. 

____

11. Mt. Washington, New Hampshire, averages $8\frac{1}{4}$ feet of rain per year. Las Vegas, Nevada, gets 4.13 inches. Which measurement is more precise? Explain.

____

____

12. In a recent August, the town Portage, Indiana had 16.67 inches of rain. The normal amount of rainfall in August is about 4 inches. Which measurement is more precise? Explain.

____

____

Name ______________________ Date ______________ Class ______________

LESSON 9-2

Practice B

Perimeter and Circumference

Find the perimeter of each polygon.

1.

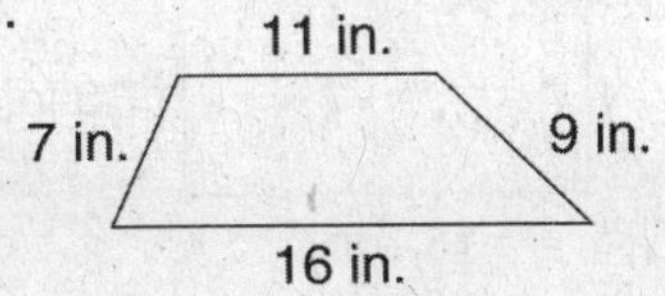

____

2.

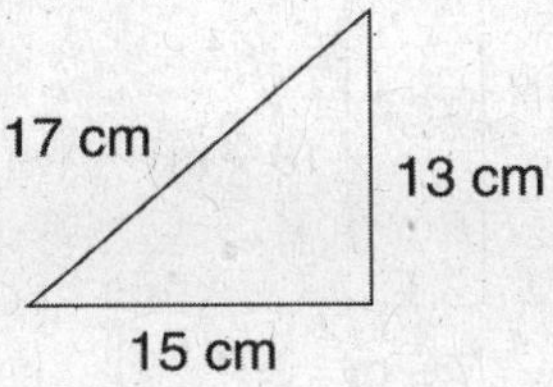

____

3.

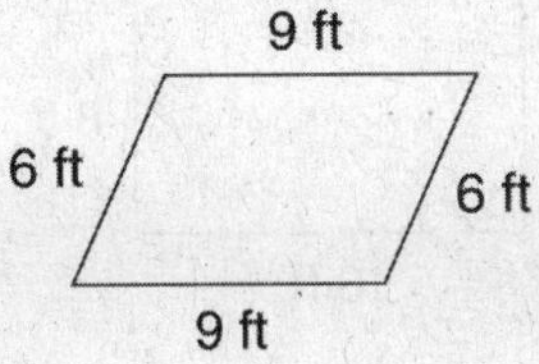

____

Find the perimeter of each rectangle.

4.

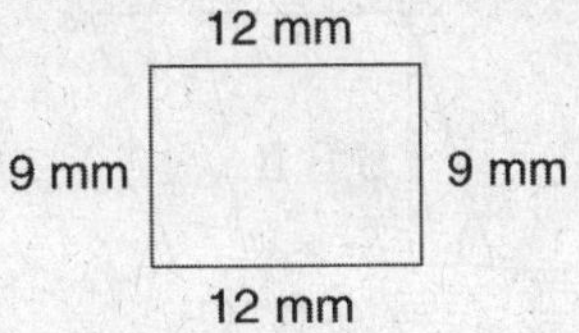

____

5.

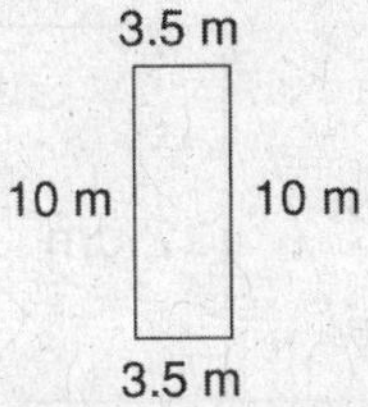

____

6.

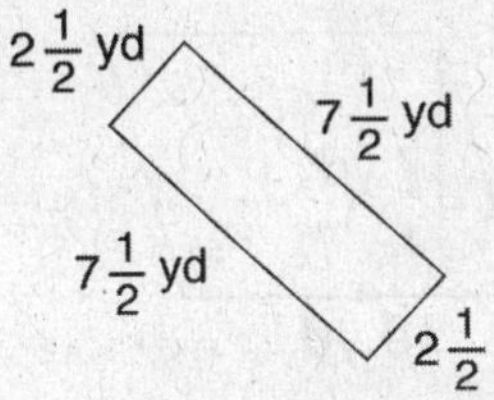

____

Find the circumference of each circle to the nearest tenth.

Use 3.14 for π or $\frac{22}{7}$.

7.

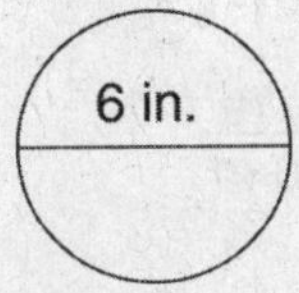

____

8.

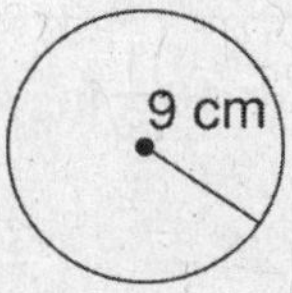

____

9.

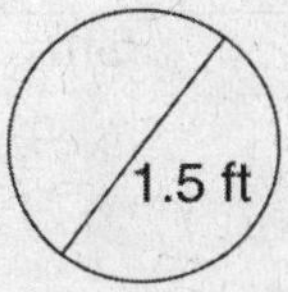

____

10. A circular swimming pool is 21 feet in diameter. What is the circumference of the swimming pool? Use $\frac{22}{7}$ for π. ______________

11. A jar lid has a diameter of 42 millimeters. What is the circumference of the lid? Use $\frac{22}{7}$ for π. ______________

12. A frying pan has a radius of 14 centimeters. What is the circumference of the frying pan? Use $\frac{22}{7}$ for π. ______________

Name ______________________ Date ______________ Class ______________

LESSON 9-3

Practice B

Area of Parallelograms

Find the area of each rectangle.

1.
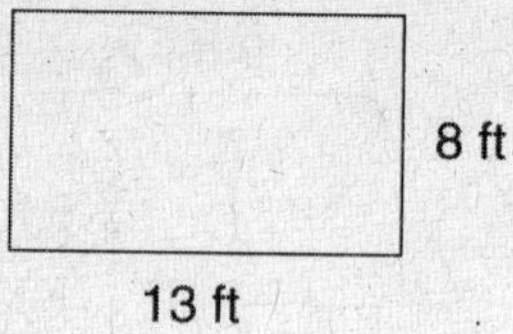

____

2.
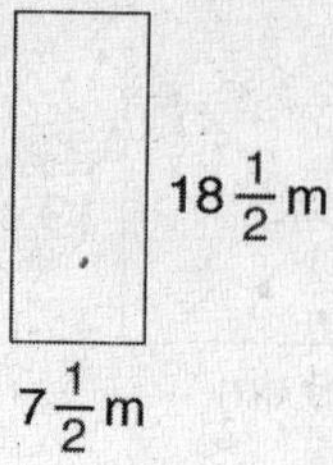

____

3.
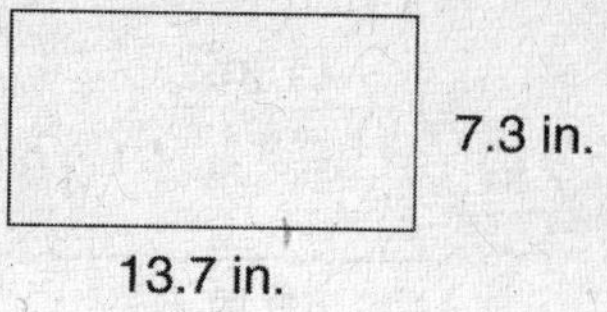

____

Find the area of each parallelogram.

4.
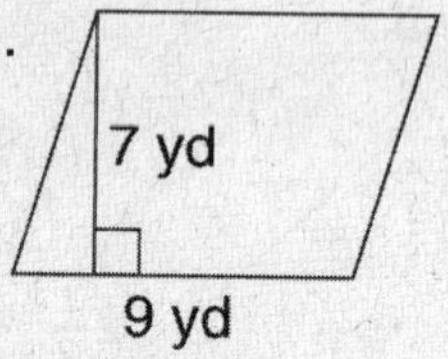

____

5
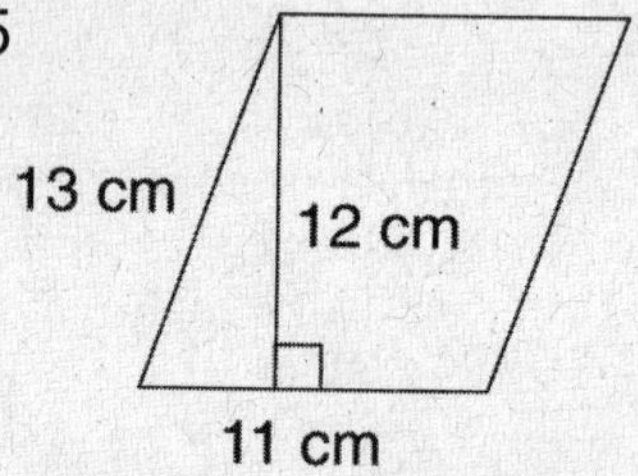

____

6.
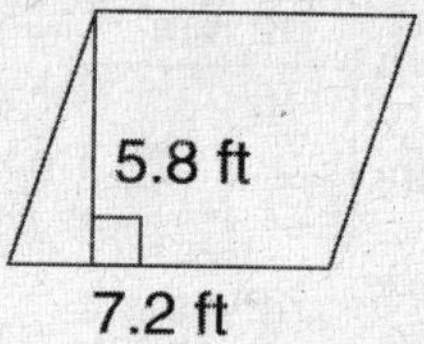

____

7.
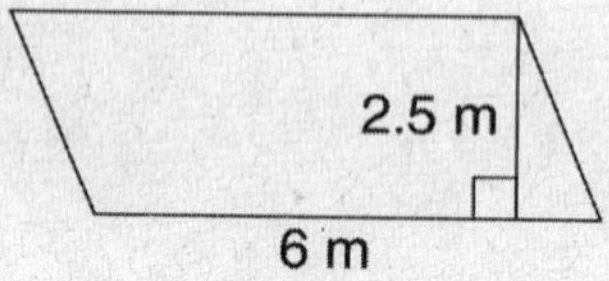

____

8.
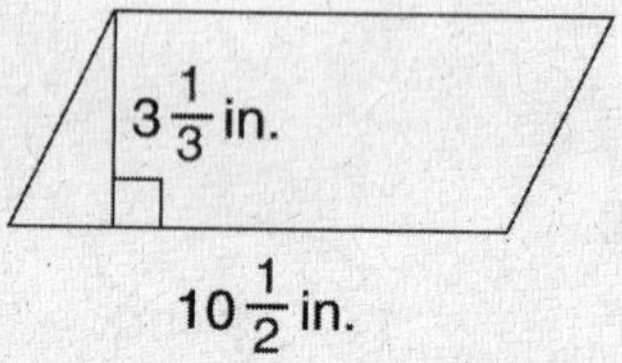

____

9.
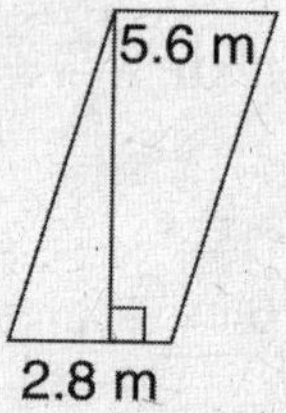

____

10. A dollar bill is 15.5 cm long and 6.5 cm wide. What is the area of a dollar bill?

____

11. A rectangular hallway has an area of 70 ft^2. The width of the hallway is 4 feet. What is the length of the hallway?

____

Name ______________________ Date ______________ Class ______________

LESSON 9-4

Practice B

Area of Triangles and Trapezoids

Find the area of each triangle.

1.

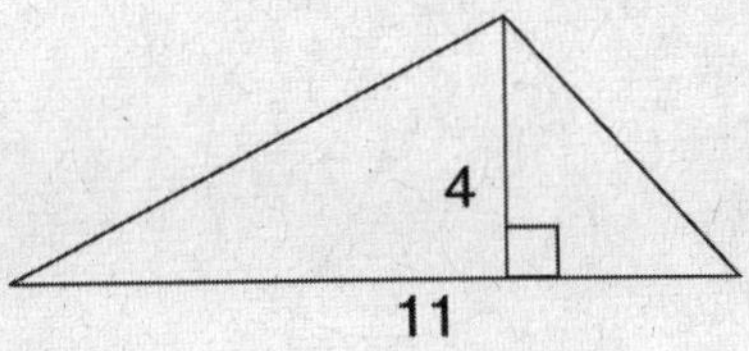

____

2.

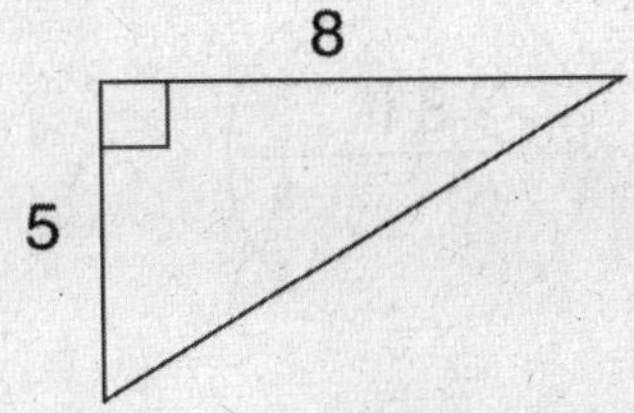

____

3.

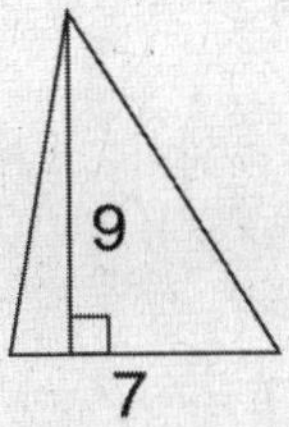

____

4.

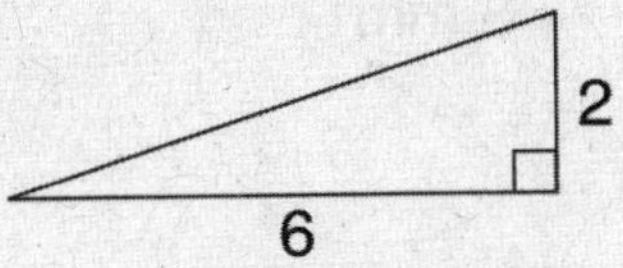

____

5.

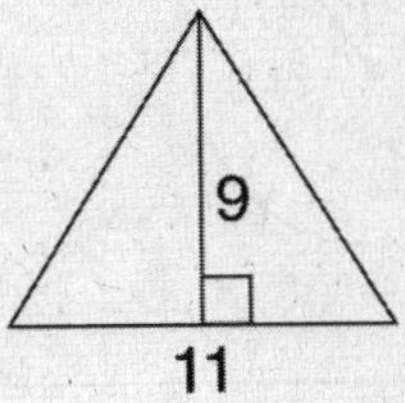

____

6.

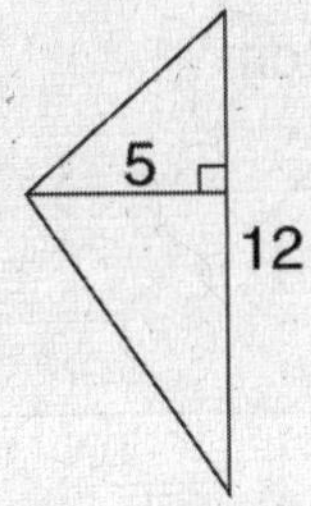

____

Find the area of each trapezoid.

7.

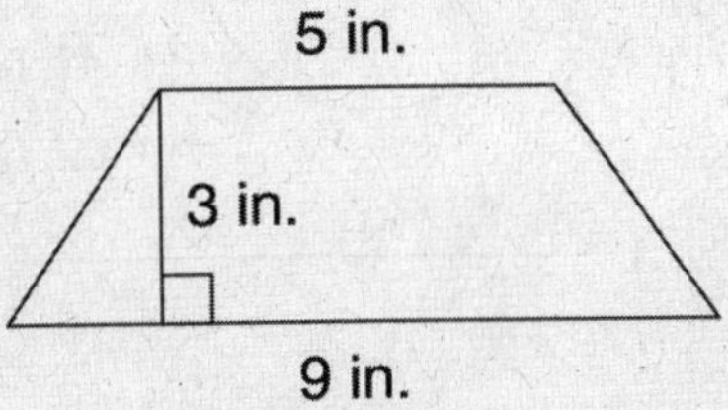

____

8.

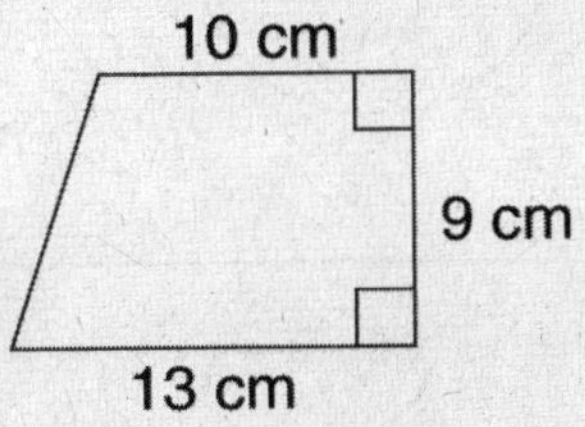

____

9.

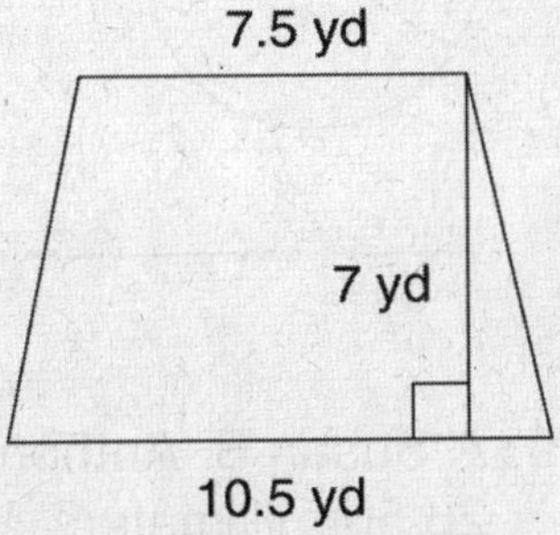

____

10.

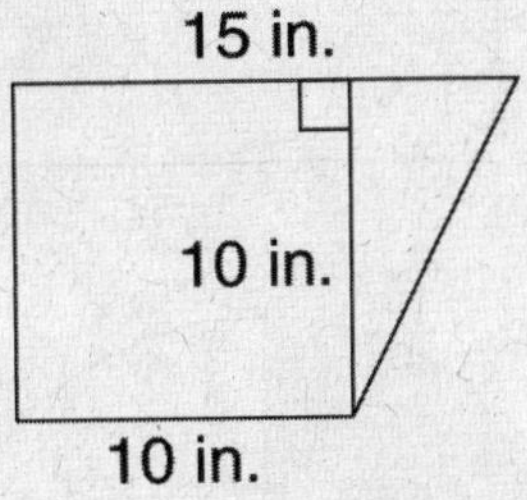

____

11.

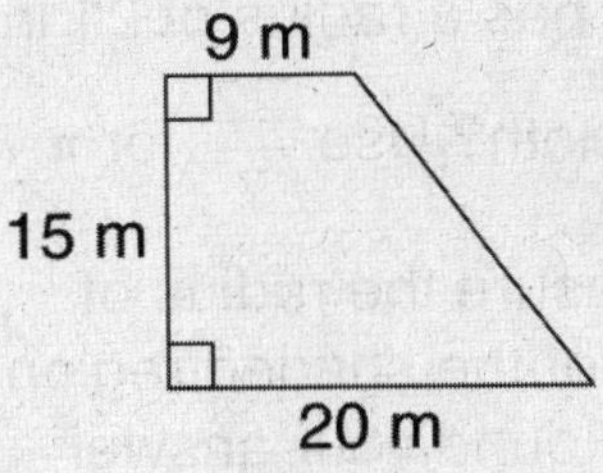

____

12.

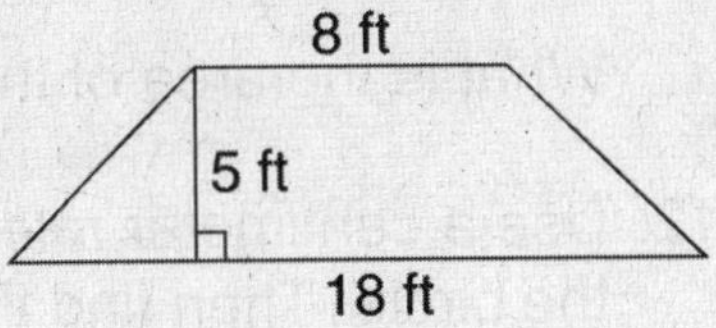

____

13. The state of Montana is shaped somewhat like a trapezoid. What is the approximate area of Montana?

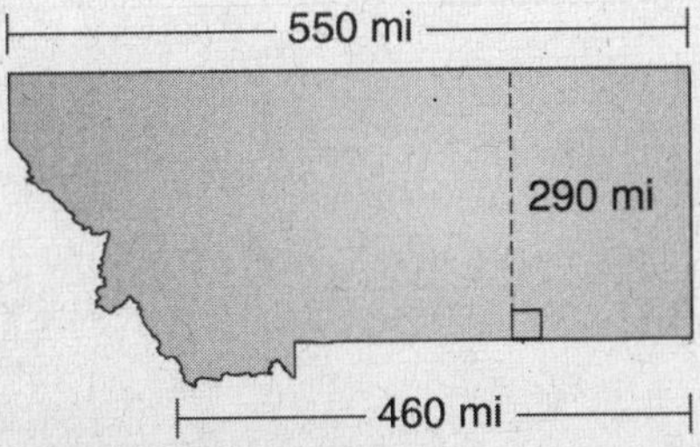

____

Name ____________________ Date ____________ Class ____________

LESSON 9-5

Practice B

Area of Circles

Find the area of each circle to the nearest tenth. Use 3.14 for π.

1.
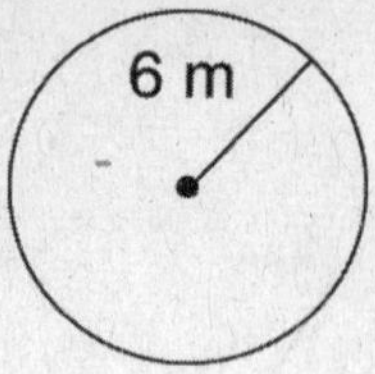

2.
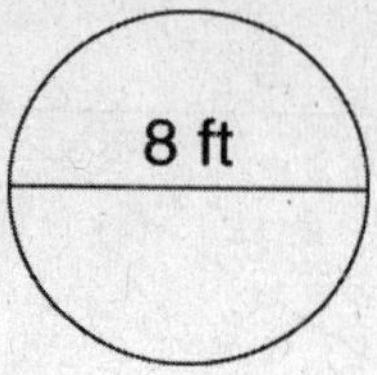

3.
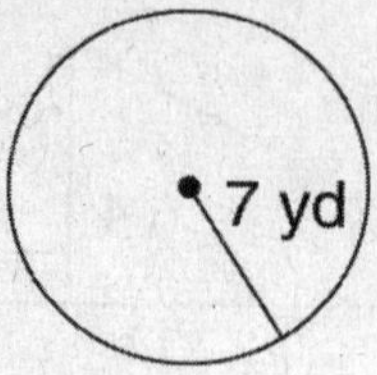

4.
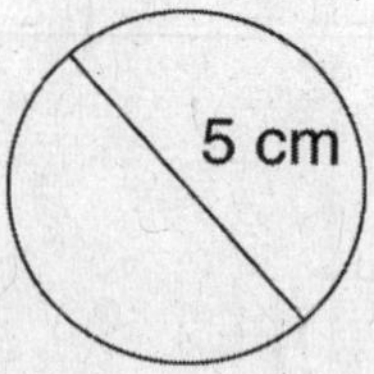

5.

6.
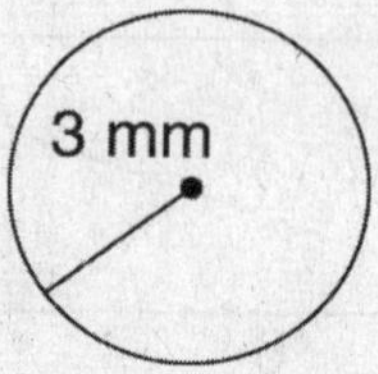

7.
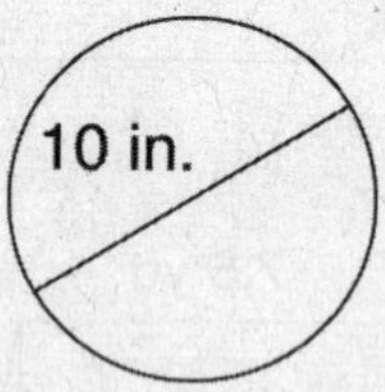

8.
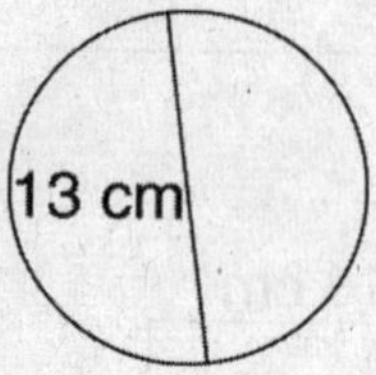

9.
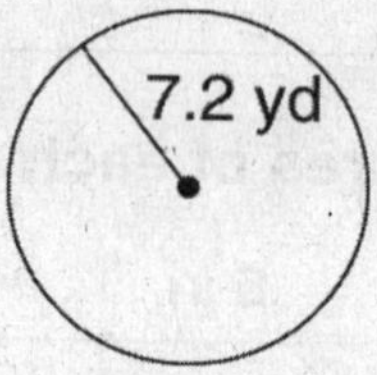

10. A Susan B. Anthony dollar coin has a diameter of 26.50 millimeters. What is the area of the coin to the nearest hundredth?

11. A tablecloth for a round table has a radius of 21 inches. What is the area of the tablecloth? Use $\frac{22}{7}$ for π.

12. Use a centimeter ruler to measure the radius of the circle. Then find the area of the shaded region of the circle. Use 3.14 for π. Round your answer to the nearest tenth.

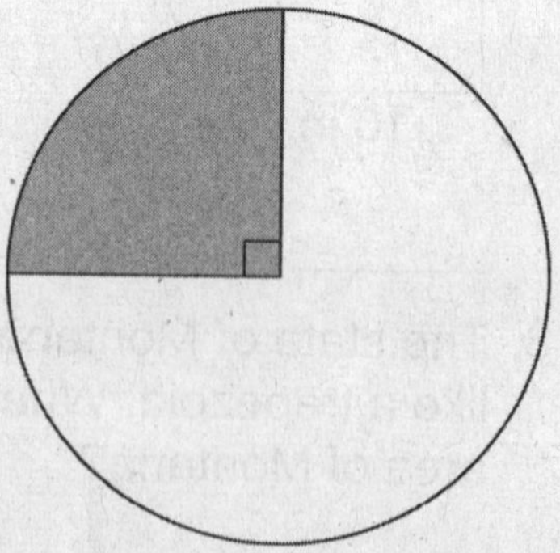

Name ______________________ Date ______________ Class ______________

LESSON 9-6

Practice A

Area of Irregular Figures

Estimate the area of each figure. Each square represents 1 square foot. Choose the letter for the best answer.

1.

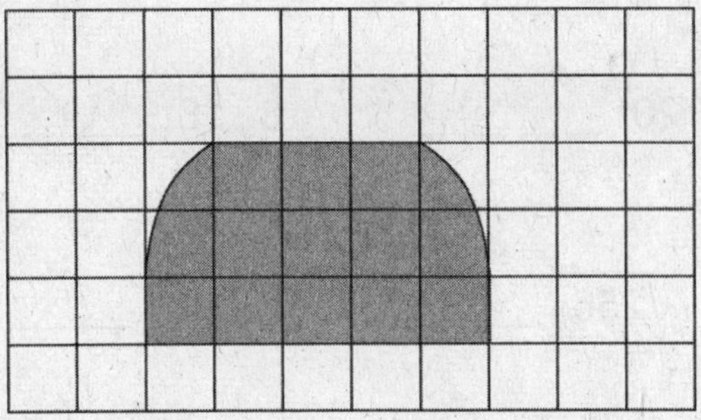

A $10\ ft^2$ C $14\ ft^2$

B $11\ ft^2$ D $15\ ft^2$

2.

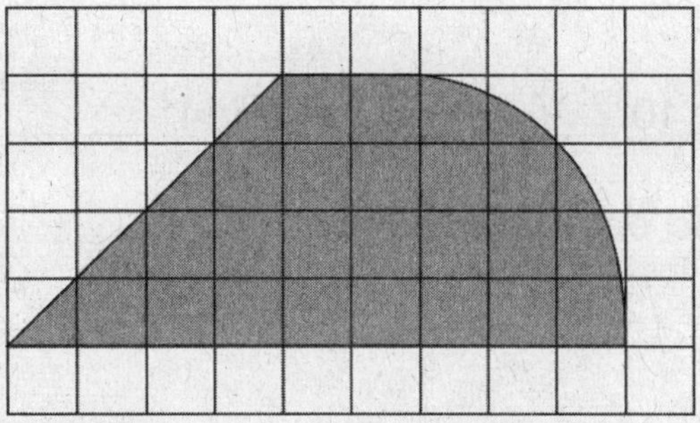

F $24\ ft^2$ H $32\ ft^2$

G $27\ ft^2$ J $36\ ft^2$

Find the area of each figure. Use 3.14 for π.

3.

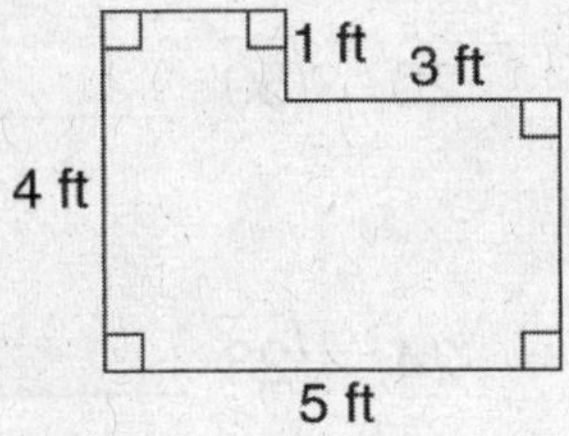

____

4.

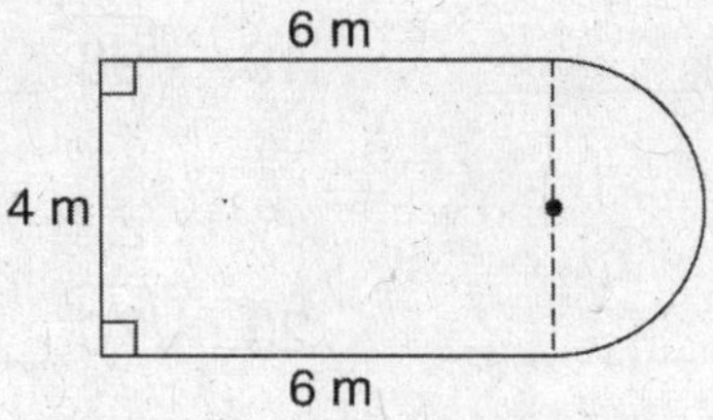

____

5.

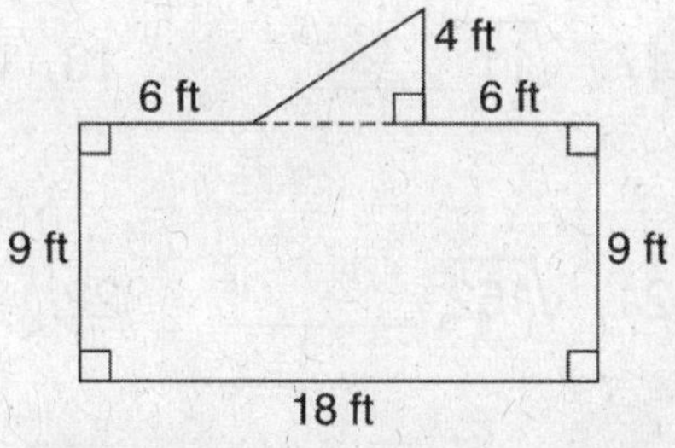

____

6.

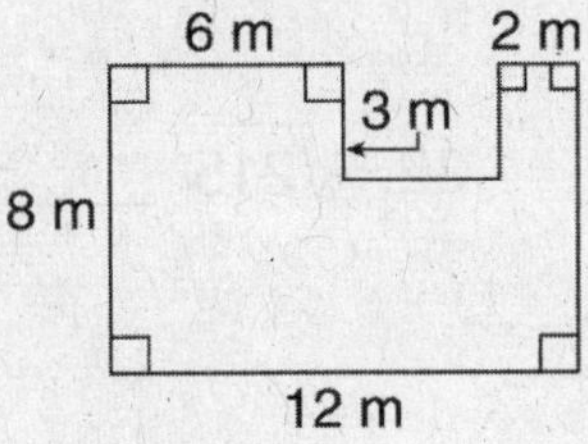

____

7.

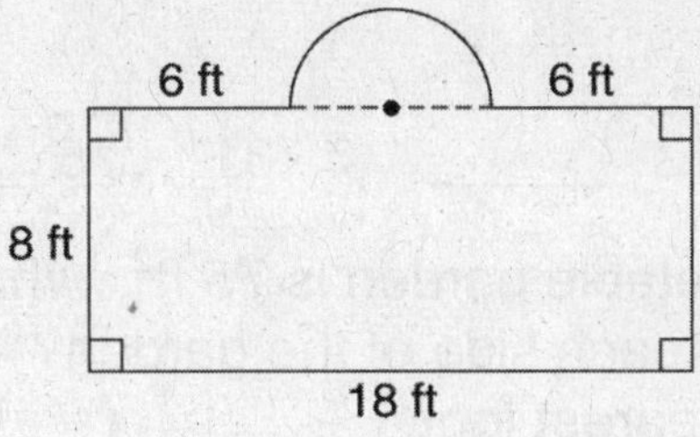

____

8.

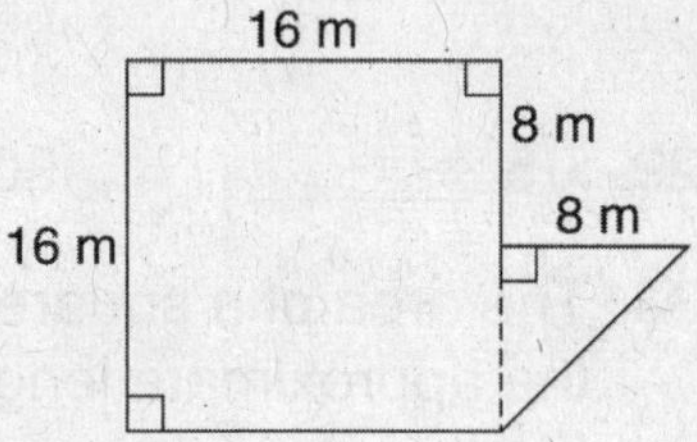

____

9. The figure shows the dimensions of a room. How much carpet is needed to cover the floor?

____

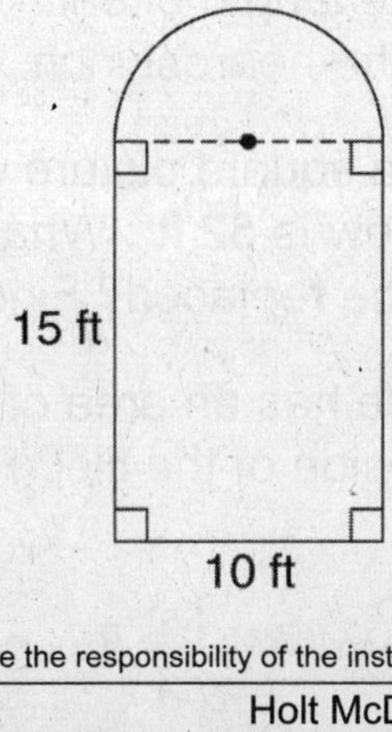

Name ______________________ Date ______________ Class ______________

LESSON 9-7

Practice B

Squares and Square Roots

Find each square.

1. 6^2 ________ 2. 19^2 ________ 3. 13^2 ________ 4. 4^2 ________

5. 10^2 ________ 6. 14^2 ________ 7. 20^2 ________ 8. 18^2 ________

Find each square root.

9. $\sqrt{289}$ ________ 10. $\sqrt{49}$ ________ 11. $\sqrt{256}$ ________ 12. $\sqrt{81}$ ________

13. $\sqrt{121}$ ________ 14. $\sqrt{625}$ ________ 15. $\sqrt{576}$ ________ 16. $\sqrt{900}$ ________

Estimate each square root to the nearest whole number. Use a calculator to check your answer.

17. $\sqrt{11}$ ______ 18. $\sqrt{31}$ ______ 19. $\sqrt{98}$ ______ 20. $\sqrt{50}$ ______

21. $\sqrt{152}$ ______ 22. $\sqrt{14}$ ______ 23. $\sqrt{70}$ ______ 24. $\sqrt{28}$ ______

25. $\sqrt{39}$ ______ 26. $\sqrt{193}$ ______ 27. $\sqrt{119}$ ______ 28. $\sqrt{85}$ ______

29. $\sqrt{5}$ ______ 30. $\sqrt{42}$ ______ 31. $\sqrt{75}$ ______ 32. $\sqrt{215}$ ______

33. The area of a square vegetable garden is 75 ft^2. What is the approximate length of each side of the garden? Find your answer to the nearest foot. ________

34. The area of a square computer screen is 138 in^2. What is the approximate length of each side of the screen? Find your answer to the nearest inch. ________

35. Tim broke a square picture window with his baseball. The area of the window is 52 ft^2. What is the approximate width of the window to be replaced? Find your answer to the nearest foot. ________

36. A square tile has an area of 413 cm^2. What is the approximate length of a side of the tile? Find your answer to the nearest centimeter. ________

Name ____________________ Date ______________ Class ______________

LESSON 9-8

Practice B

The Pythagorean Theorem

Use the Pythagorean Theorem to find each missing measure.

1.

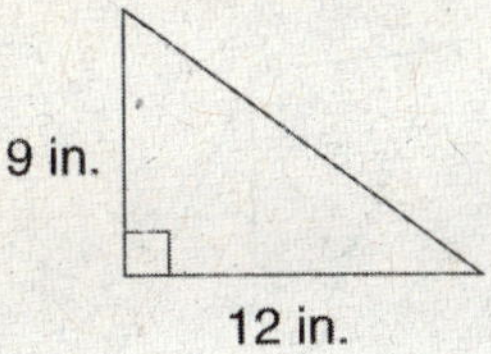

____

2.

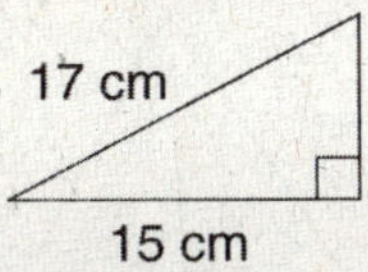

____

3.

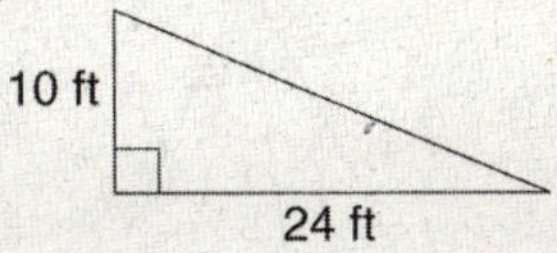

____

4.

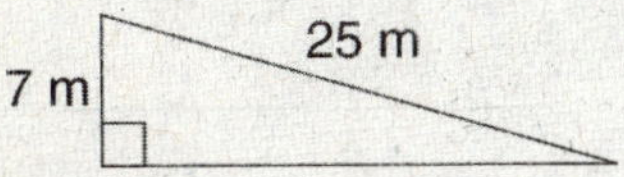

____

5.

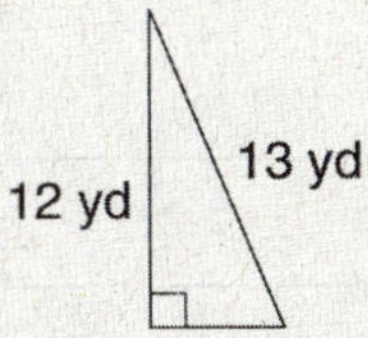

____

6.

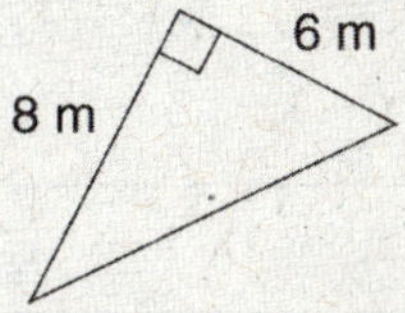

____

7.

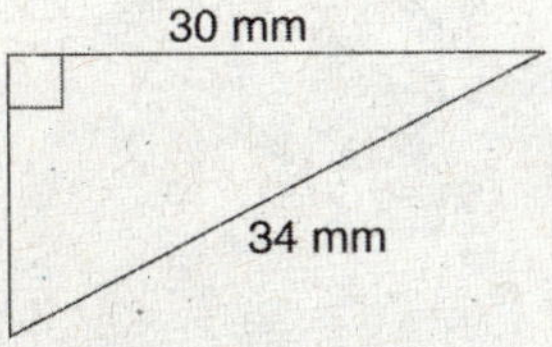

____

8.

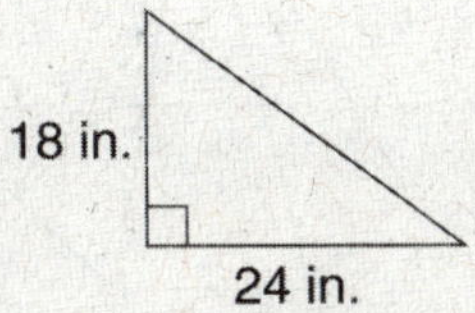

____

9.

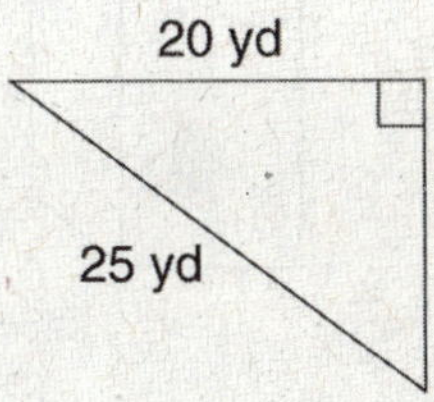

____

10. A 20-ft ladder is leaning against a wall. If the ladder is 12 ft from the base of the wall, how high above the ground does the ladder touch the wall? ______________

11. A checkerboard is 10 inches long on each side. What is the length of the diagonal from one corner to another? Round your answer to the nearest tenth. ______________

12. Chang lives 8 miles east of the school. Deborah lives 12 miles south of the school. Approximately how far apart are Chang's and Deborah's homes? Round your answer to the nearest tenth. ______________

13. A rectangle is 26 meters long and 18 meters wide. What is the length of the diagonal of the rectangle to the nearest meter? ______________

Name ______________________ Date ______________ Class ______________

LESSON 10-1

Practice B

Introduction to Three-Dimensional Figures

Identify the bases and faces of each figure. Then name the figure.

1. 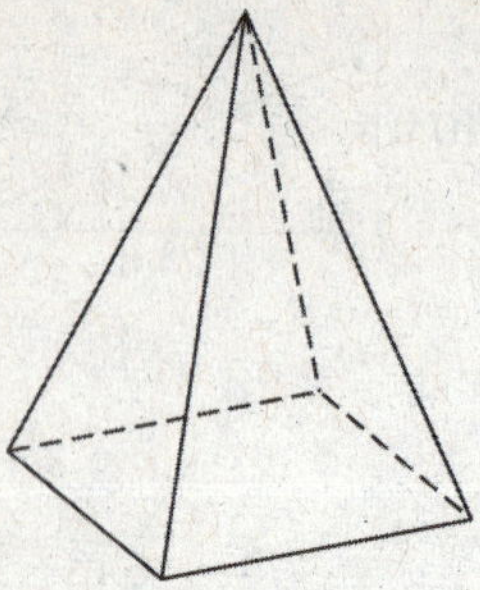

2. 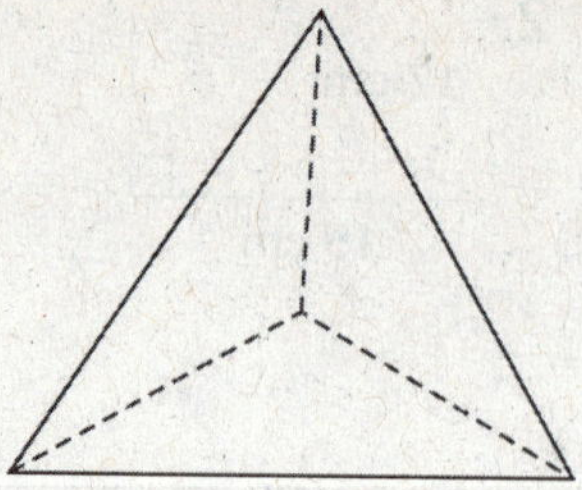

3. 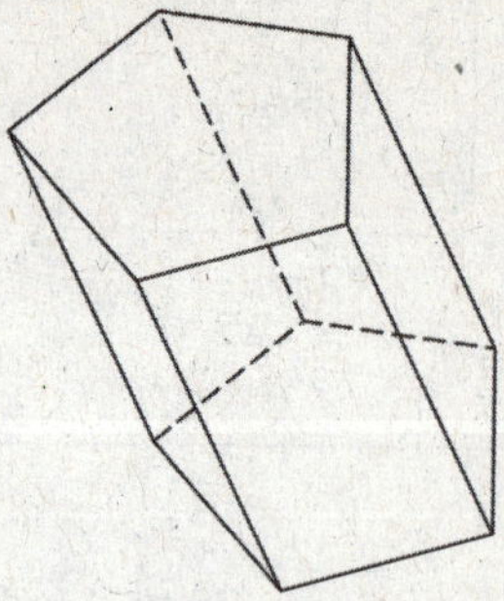

4. 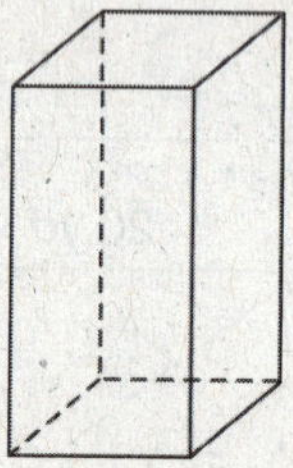

5. 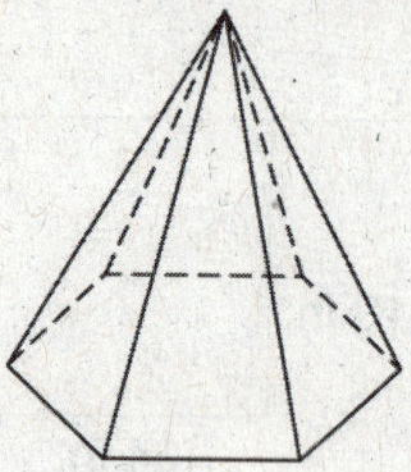

6. 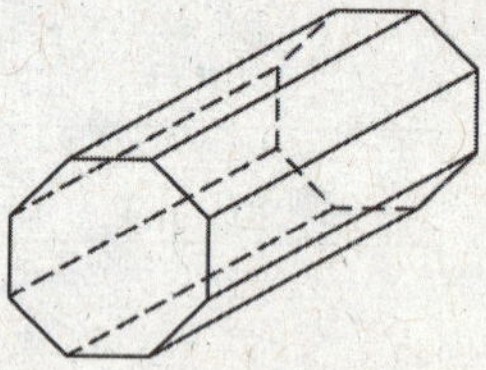

Classify each figure as a polyhedron or not a polyhedron. Then name the figure.

7. 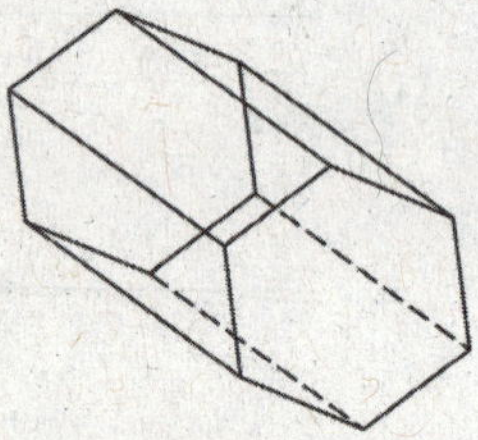

8. 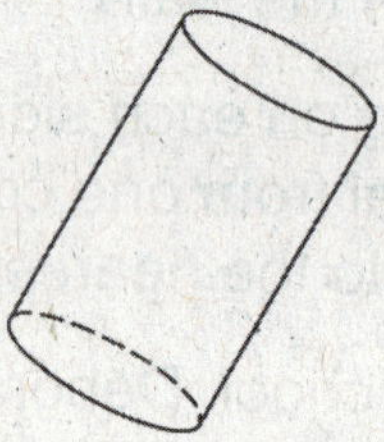

9. 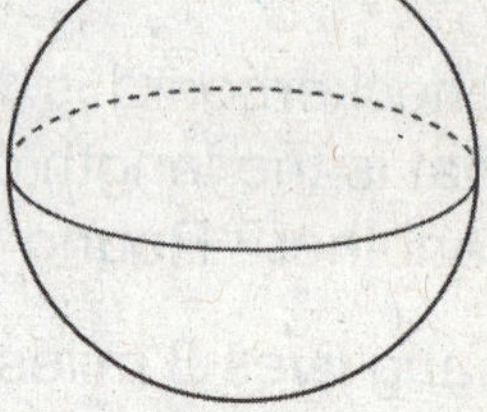

10. 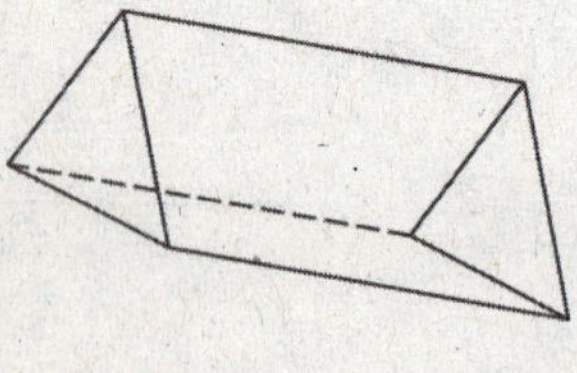

11. 

12. 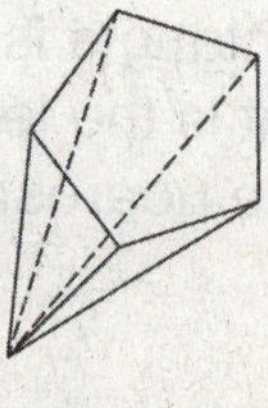

Name ______________________ Date ____________ Class ____________

LESSON 10-2

Practice B

Volume of Prisms and Cylinders

Find the volume of each figure.

1.

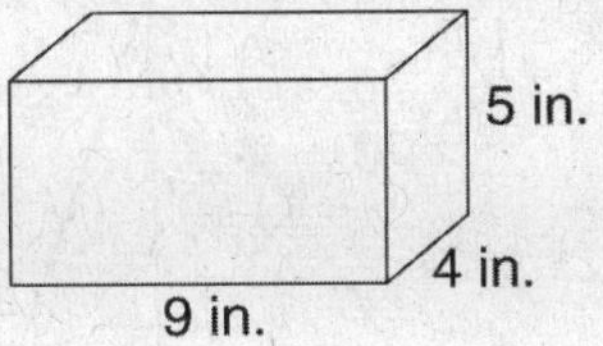

2.

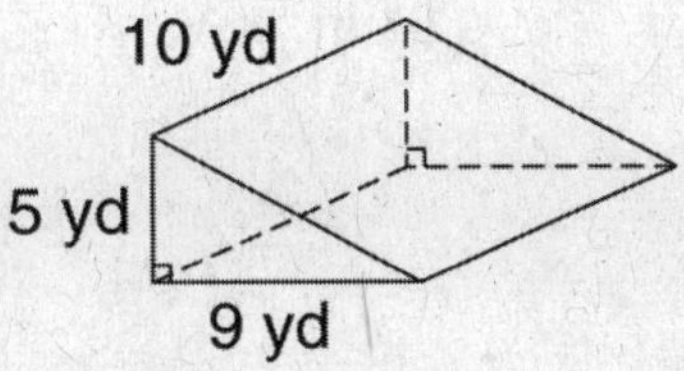

3.

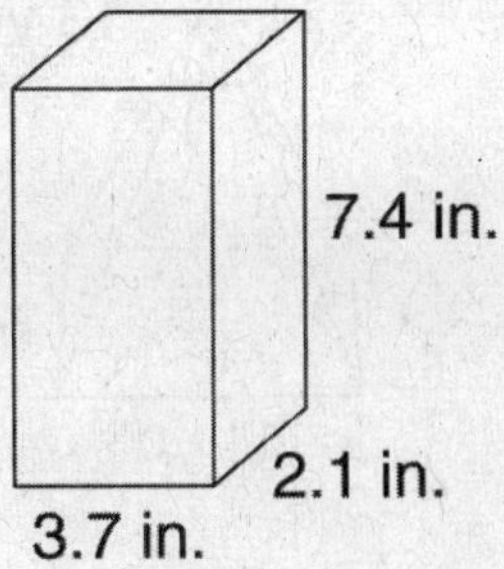

4.

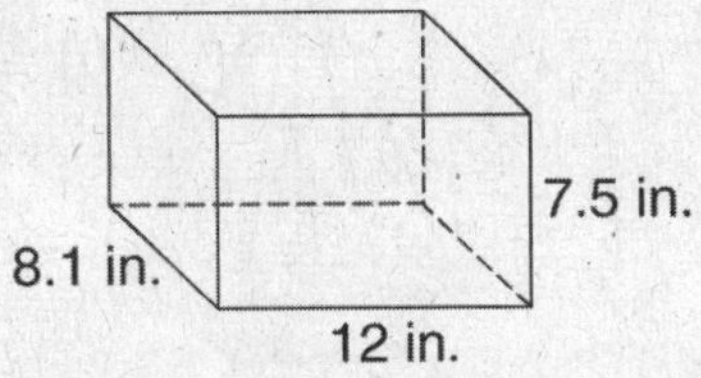

5.

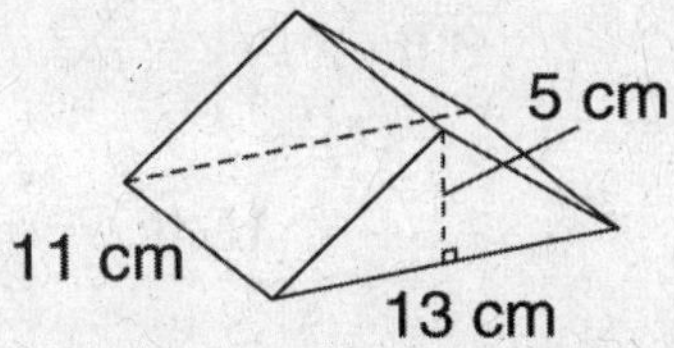

6.

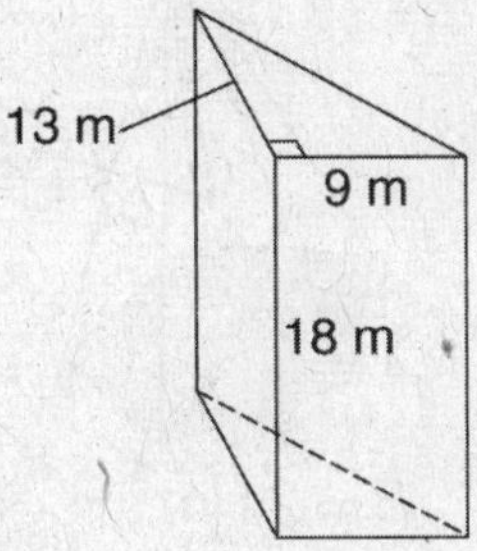

7. A travel mug is shaped like a cylinder. It is 9 centimeters wide and 15 centimeters tall. Find its volume to the nearest tenth. Use 3.14 for π.

Find the volume of the composite figure to the nearest tenth. Use 3.14 for π.

8.

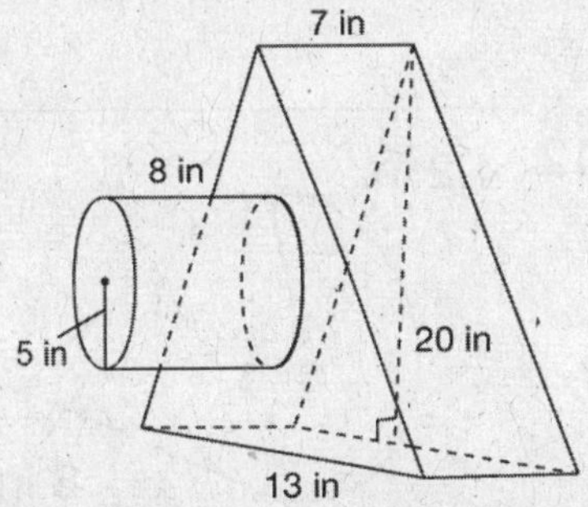

9.

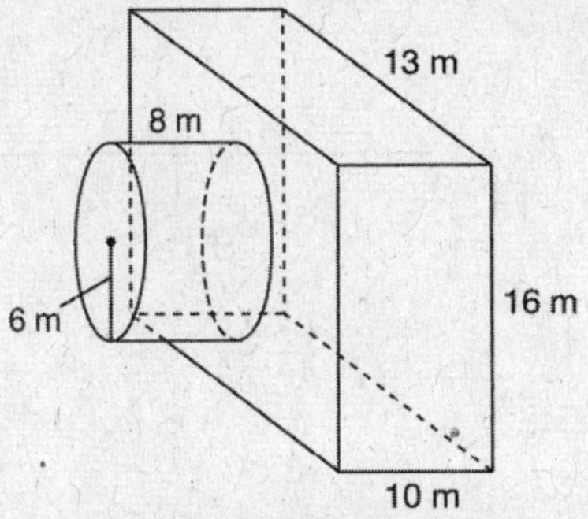

10.

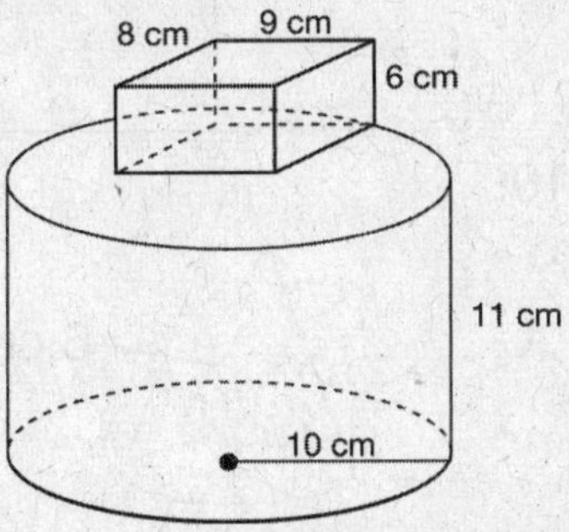

Name ______________________ Date ____________ Class ____________

LESSON 10-3

Practice B

Volume of Pyramids and Cones

Find the volume of each pyramid to the nearest tenth.

1.

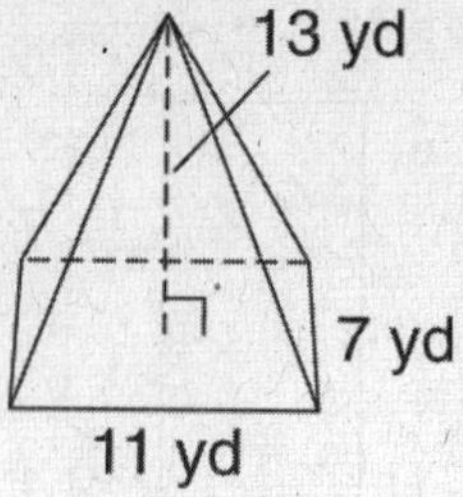

____

2.

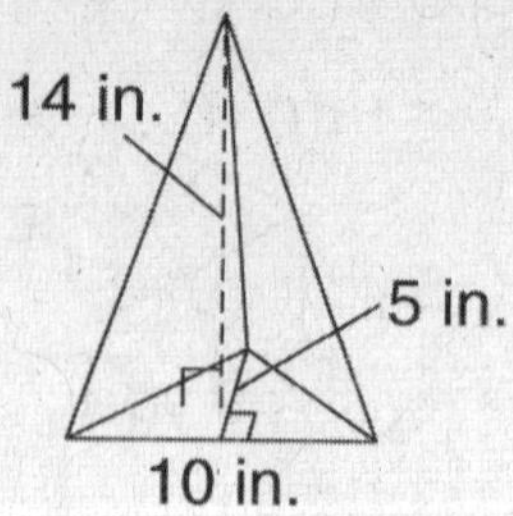

____

3.

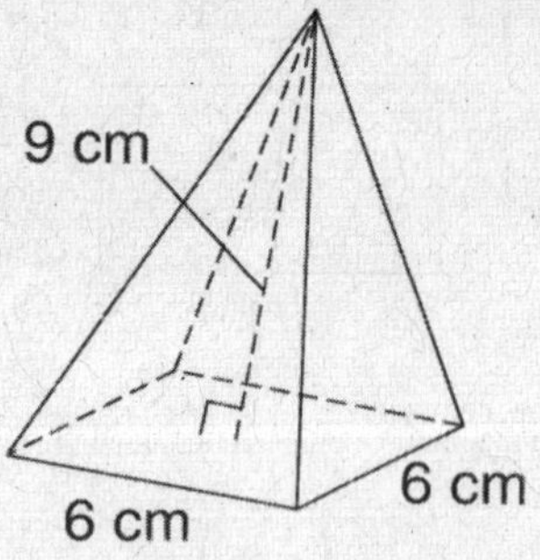

____

4.

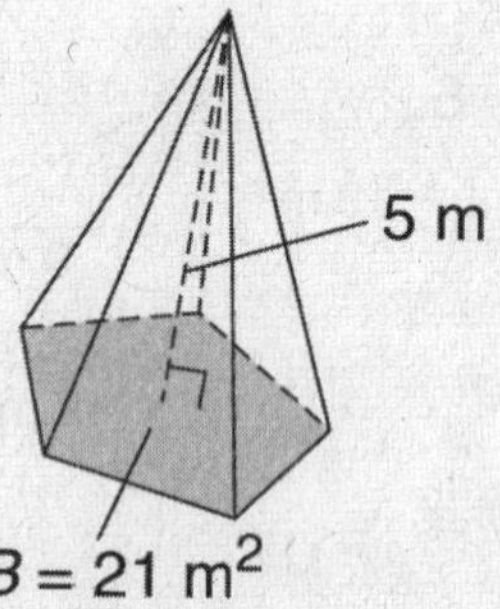

____

5.

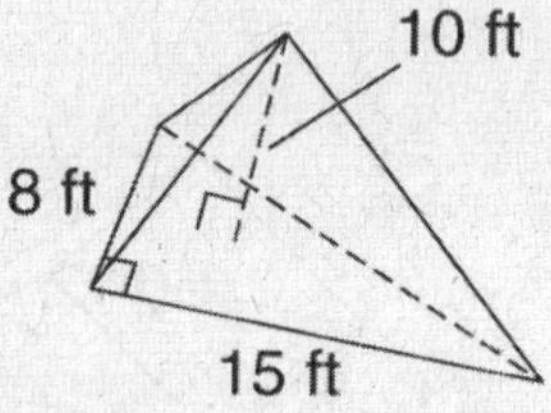

____

6.

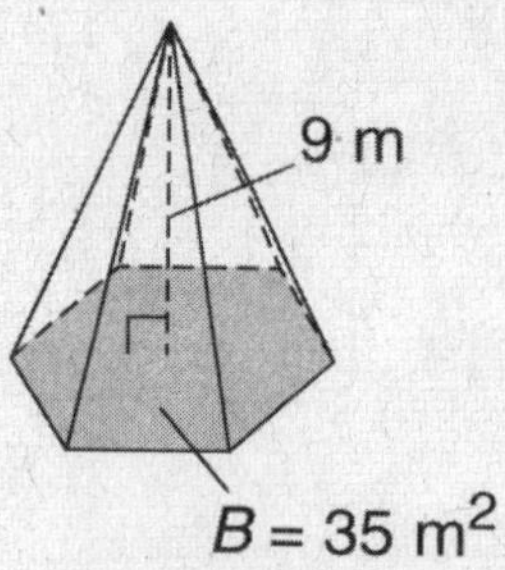

____

Find the volume of each cone to the nearest tenth. Use 3.14 for π.

7.

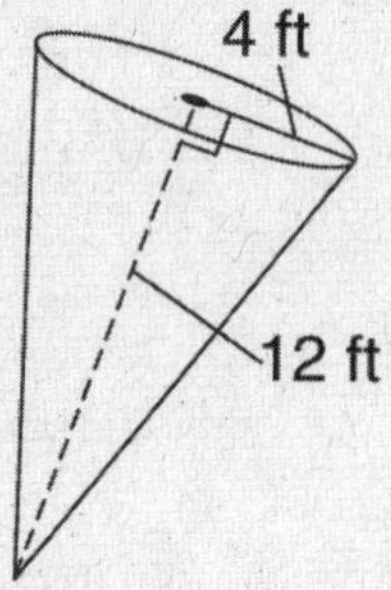

____

8.

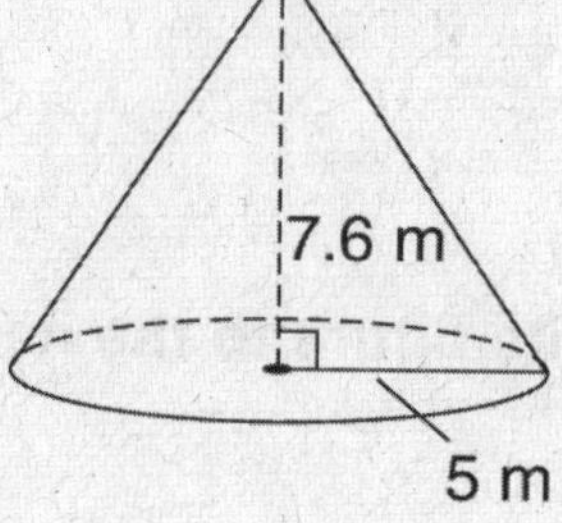

____

9.

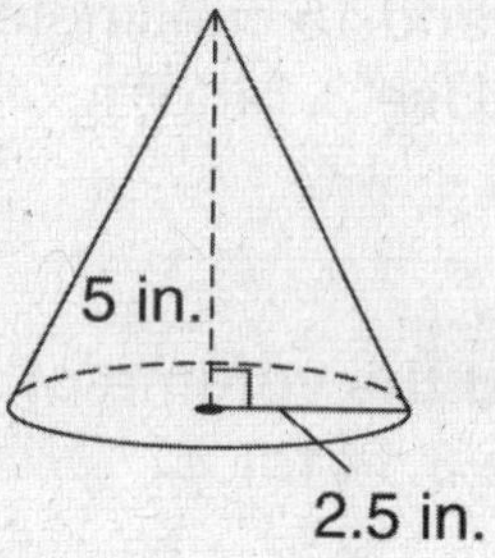

____

10.

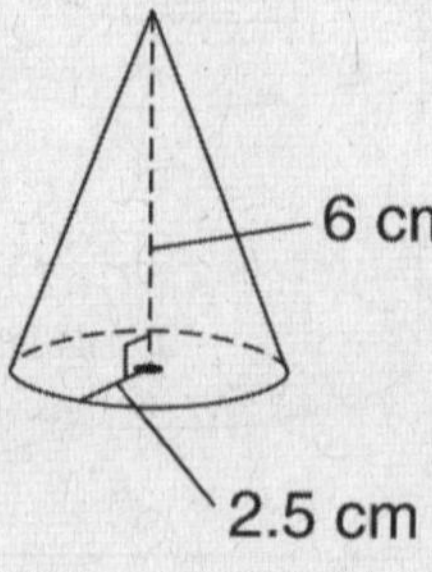

____

11.

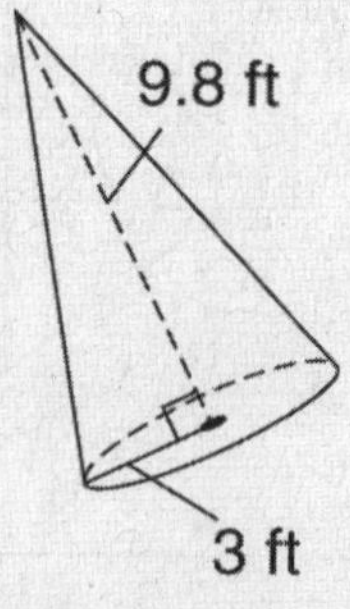

____

12.

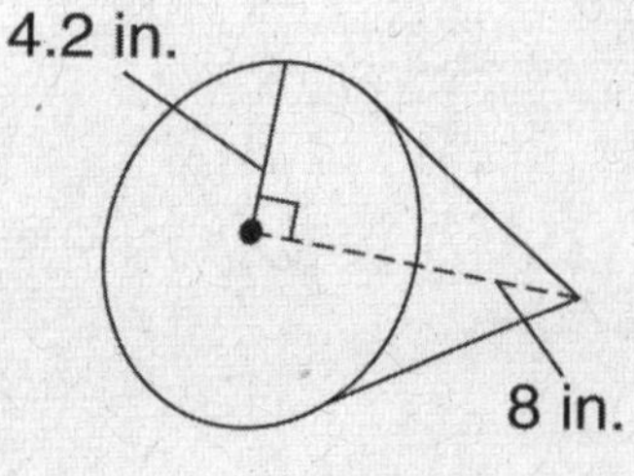

____

Name ______________________ Date ______________ Class ______________

LESSON 10-4

Practice B

Surface Area of Prisms and Cylinders

Find the surface area of each prism to the nearest tenth.

1.

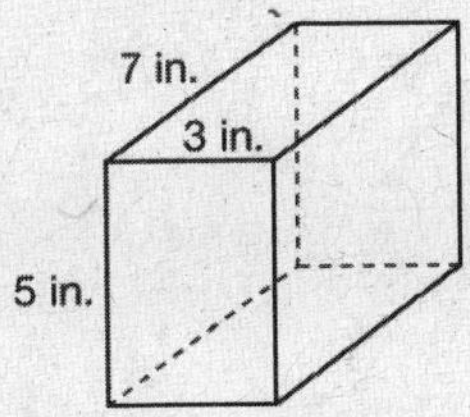

____

2.

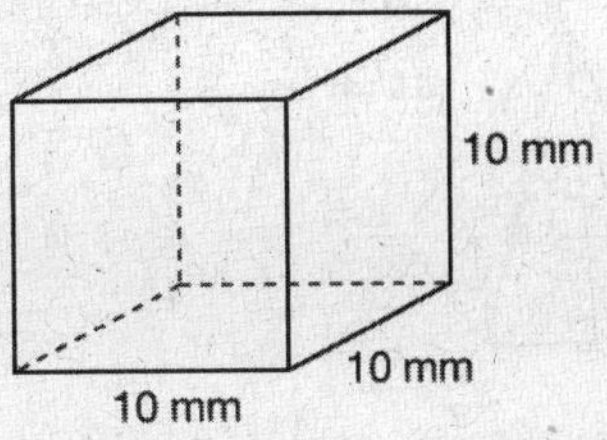

____

Find the surface area of each cylinder to the nearest tenth.

3.

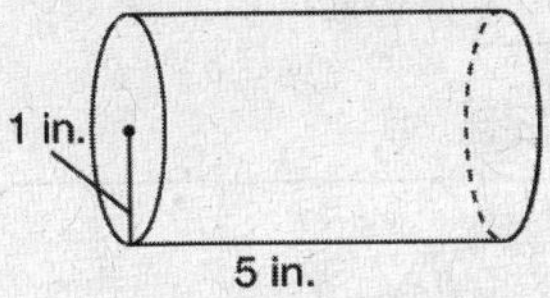

____

4.

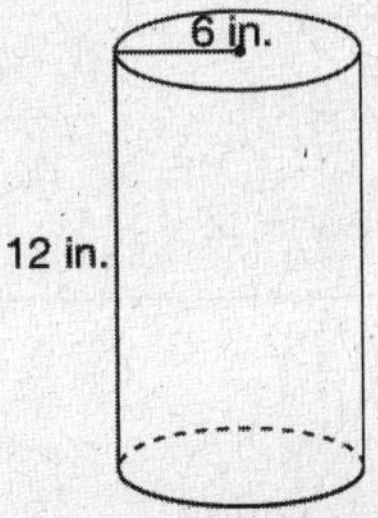

____

5. Trina is designing a tent with the dimensions shown. What is the surface area of the tent? Round to the nearest tenth.

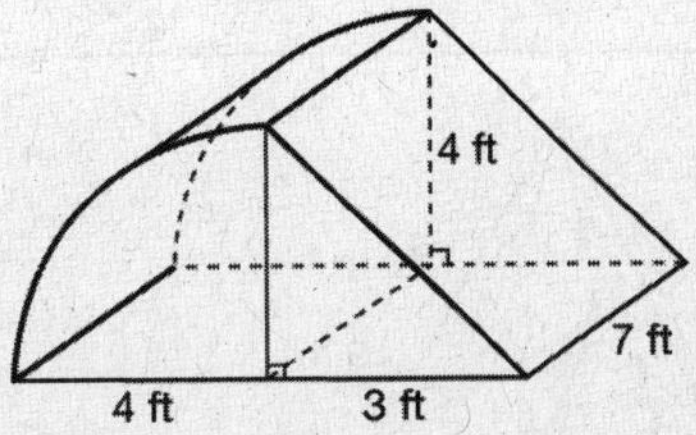

____

Name ______________________ Date ______________ Class ______________

LESSON 10-5

Practice B

Surface Area of Pyramids and Cones

Find the surface area of each pyramid.

1.
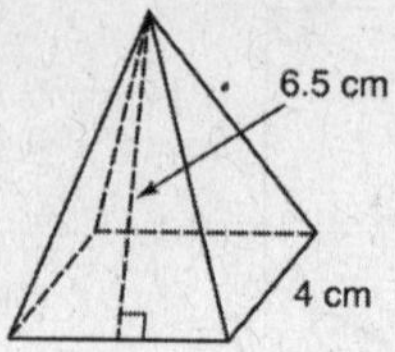

____

2.
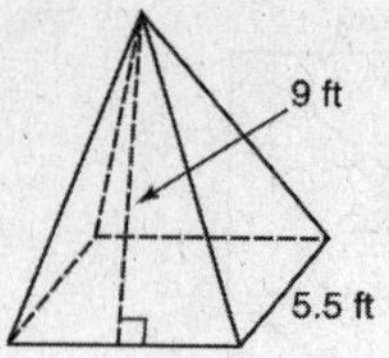

____

3.
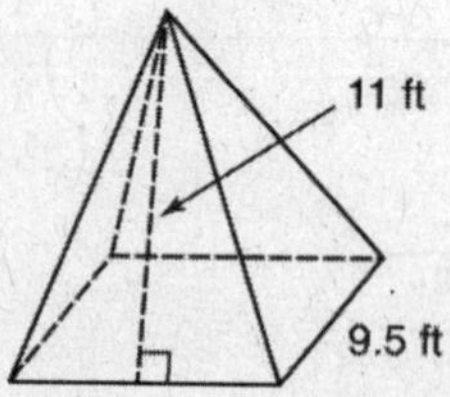

____

4.
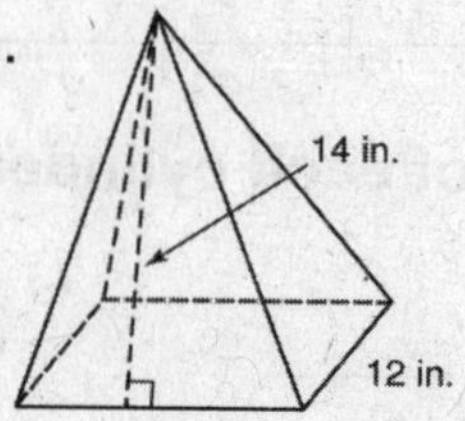

____

5.
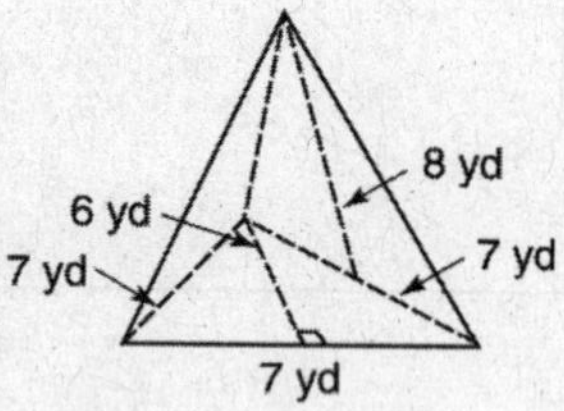

____

6.
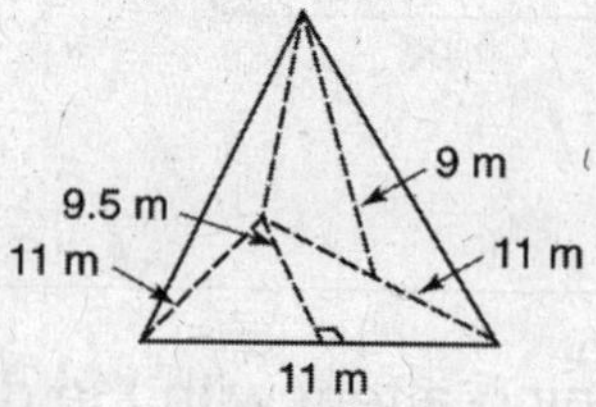

____

7.
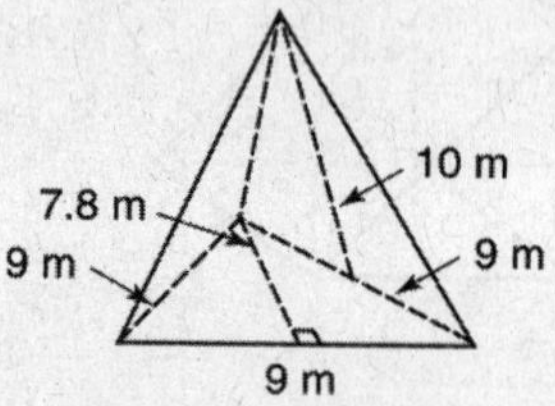

____

8.
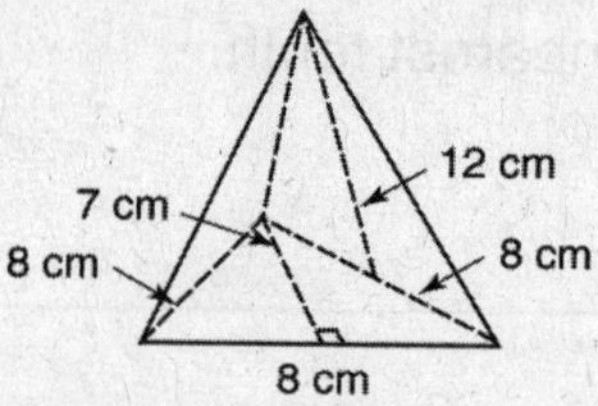

____

Find the surface area of each cone. Use 3.14 for π.

9.
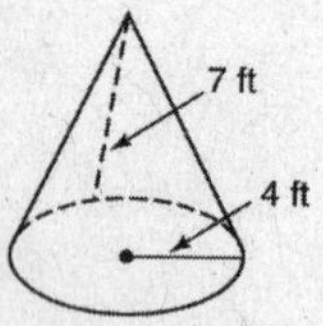

____

10.
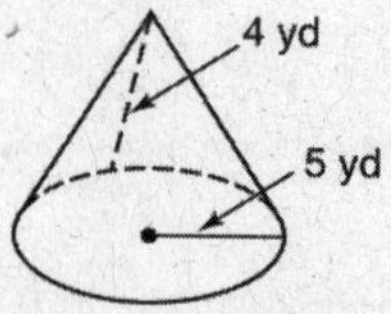

____

11.
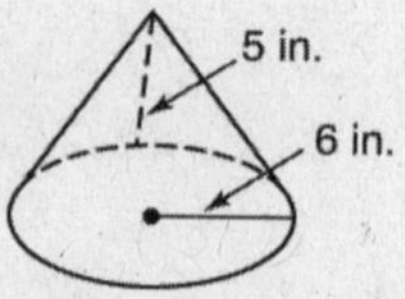

____

12.
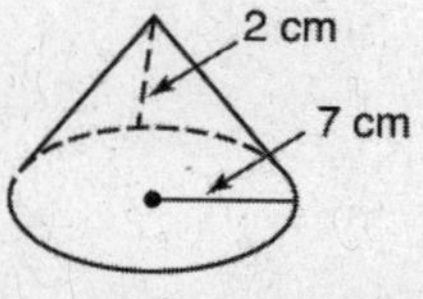

____

Name ______________________ Date ______________ Class ______________

LESSON 10-6

Practice B

Changing Dimensions

Given the scale factor, find the surface area of the similar prism.

1. The scale factor of two similar rectangular prisms is 3. The surface area of the smaller prism is 15 in^2. ______________
2. The scale factor of two similar triangular prisms is 2. The surface area of the smaller prism is 25 cm^2. ______________
3. The scale factor of two similar rectangular prisms is $\frac{1}{2}$. The surface area of the larger prism is 960 ft^2. ______________
4. The scale factor of two similar triangular prisms is 5. The surface area of the smaller prism is 10 m^2. ______________
5. The scale factor of two similar rectangular prisms is $\frac{1}{5}$. The surface area of the larger prism is 625 in^2. ______________
6. The scale factor of two similar pentagonal prisms is 4. The surface area of the smaller prism is 16 cm^2. ______________

Given the scale factor, find the volume of the similar prism.

7. The scale factor of two similar triangular prisms is 3. The volume of the smaller prism is 8 in^3. ______________
8. The scale factor of two similar rectangular prisms is $\frac{1}{2}$. The volume of the larger prism is 648 m^3. ______________
9. The scale factor of two similar triangular prisms is 4. The volume of the smaller prism is 10 cm^3. ______________
10. The scale factor of two similar rectangular prisms is $\frac{1}{4}$. The volume of the larger prism is 1,920 ft^3. ______________
11. The scale factor of two similar triangular prisms is 2. The volume of the smaller prism is 72 yd^3. ______________
12. A small tank weighs 24 pounds when it is full of water. A larger tank that is similar in shape has a scale factor of 3. How much does the larger tank weigh when filled with water? ______________

Name ______________________ Date ______________ Class ______________

LESSON 11-1

Practice B

Probability

Determine whether each event is impossible, unlikely, as likely as not, likely, or certain.

1. rolling an even number on a number cube labeled 1 through 6 ______________
2. picking a card with a vowel on it from a box of cards in which each letter of the alphabet is written on a card ______________
3. spinning a number greater than 2 on a spinner with 10 equal sections marked 1 through 10 ______________
4. drawing a red marble from a bag of black, blue, and green marbles ______________
5. flipping a coin and getting heads or tails ______________
6. rolling a number that is less than three 5 times in a row on a number cube labeled 1 through 6 ______________

Solve.

7. A bag contains 3 green marbles, 7 blue marbles, and 2 black marbles. The probability of randomly picking a green marble is $\frac{1}{4}$. What is the probability of not picking a green marble? ______________
8. A spinner has 8 equal sections labeled 1 through 8. The probability of spinning a number that is greater than or equal to 6 is $\frac{3}{8}$. What is the probability of spinning a number that is not greater than or equal to 6? ______________
9. The probability of randomly drawing a red card from a bag that contains red, blue, and green cards is $\frac{3}{10}$. What is the probability of not drawing a red card? ______________
10. Myra almost always spends at least 45 minutes on the treadmill. If Myra got on the treadmill at 5:20 P.M., estimate the probability that she will still be on the treadmill at 6:00. ______________
11. Morris rarely arrives home before 4:00 P.M. It is now 3:20 P.M. Estimate the probability that Morris will arrive home in the next 30 minutes. ______________

Name ______________________ Date ______________ Class ______________

LESSON 11-2

Practice B

Experimental Probability

Find the experimental probability. Write your answer as a fraction, as a decimal, and as percent.

1. Jaclyn is a soccer goalie. If she has 21 out of 25 saves in practice, what is the experimental probability that she will have a save on the next shot on goal? ______________

2. If Harris hit the bull's-eye 3 out of 8 times at archery practice, what is the experimental probability that he will hit the bull's-eye on his next try? ______________

3. Nathan inspects new pants at a factory. Of the first 56 pairs of pants he inspected 49 were acceptable. What is the experimental probability that the next pair of pants will be acceptable? ______________

4. Sara has gone to work for 60 days. On 39 of those days she arrived at work before 8:30 A.M. On the rest of the days she arrived after 8:30 A.M. What is the experimental probability that she will arrive at work after 8:30 A.M. the next day she goes to work? ______________

Solve.

5. After a movie premiere, 99 of the first 130 people surveyed said they liked the movie.

   a. What is the experimental probability that the next person surveyed will say he or she liked the movie? ______________

   b. What is the experimental probability that the next person surveyed will say he or she did not like the movie? ______________

6. For the past 30 days, Naomi has been recording the number of customers at her restaurant between 10 A.M. and 11 A.M. During that hour, there have been fewer than 20 customers on 25 out of 30 days.

   a. What is the experimental probability that there will be fewer than 20 customers on the thirty-first day? ______________

   b. What is the experimental probability that there will be 20 or more customers on the thirty-first day? ______________

7. For the past four weeks, Nestor has been recording the daily high temperatures. During that time, the high temperature has been below 45° on 20 out of 28 days. What is the experimental probability that the high temperature will be below 45° on the twenty-ninth day? ______________

Name ______________________ Date ______________ Class ______________

LESSON 11-3

Practice B

Sample Spaces

1. Marcus spins the spinner at the right and flips a dime at the same time. What are the possible outcomes? How many outcomes are in the sample space?

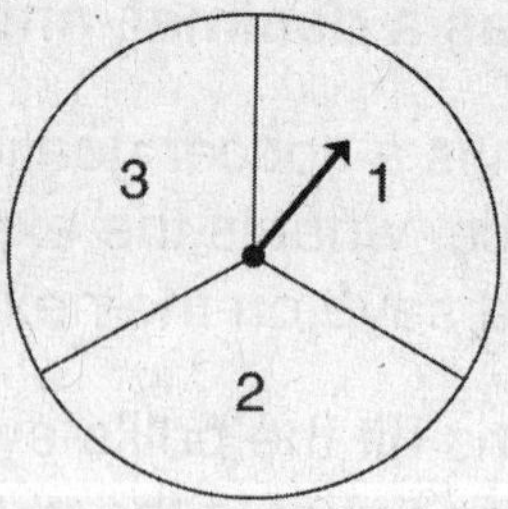

____

____

2. For lunch, Britney has a choice of a hot dog, a hamburger, or pizza and a choice of an apple, a pear, or grapes. What are all the possible choices of lunch she can have? How many outcomes are in the sample space?

____

____

____

____

3. Susan and Ryan are playing a game that involves spinning the spinner at the right and flipping a penny. How many outcomes are possible in the game?

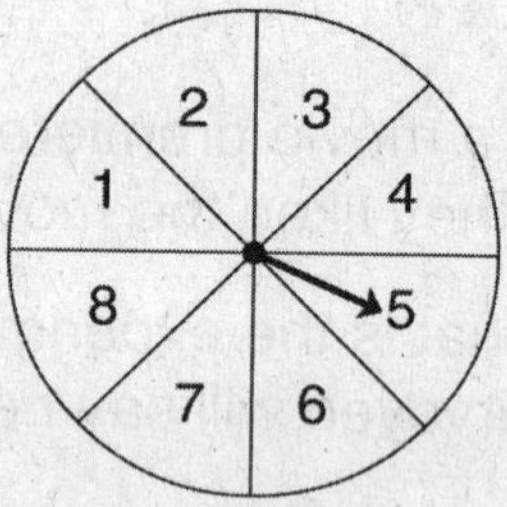

____

4. An Italian restaurant offers small, medium, and large calzones. The choices of fillings are cheese, sausage, spinach, or vegetable. How many different calzones can you order?

____

5. There are 5 ways to go from Town X to Town Y. There are 3 ways to go from Town Y to Town Z. How many different ways are there to go from Town X to Town Z, passing through Town Y?

____

6. Rasheed has tan pants, black pants, gray pants, and blue pants. He has a brown sweater and a white sweater. How many different ways can he wear a sweater and pants together?

____

Name ______________________ Date ____________ Class ____________

LESSON 11-4

Practice B

Theoretical Probability

Find the probability of each event. Write your answer as a fraction, as a decimal, and as a percent. Round to the nearest tenth of a percent.

1. randomly choosing a white counter from a bag of 12 red counters, 12 white counters, 12 green counters, and 12 blue counters

____

2. tossing two fair coins and having one land on tails and one land on heads

____

3. rolling a number greater than 1 on a fair number cube

____

4. randomly choosing an orange disk from a bag of 14 black disks, 4 blue disks and 12 orange disks

____

5. randomly choosing 1 of the 6 R's from a bag of 100 letter tiles

____

6. spinning a number less than 7 on a fair spinner with 8 equal sections labeled 1–8

____

A set of cards has 20 cards with stars, 10 cards with squares, and 15 cards with circles. Find the probability of each event when a card is chosen at random.

7. square ____________

8. circle ____________

9. star or circle ____________

10. not circle or square ____________

There are 14 girls and 18 boys in Ms. Wiley's class. Ms. Wiley randomly selects one student to solve a problem. Find the probability of each event.

11. selecting a boy ____________

12. selecting a girl ____________

Name ______________________ Date ______________ Class ______________

LESSON 11-5

Practice B

Making Predictions

Make a prediction based on an experimental probability.

1. A baseball player reaches base 35% of the time. How many times can he expect to reach base in 850 at-bats?

____

2. Fredericka can make 65% of her shots from the free-throw line. If she shoots 75 times, how many shots can she expect to go in?

____

3. In 1951, Odessa, Texas had temperatures of at least 95° F 11% of the time. During that year, how many days could residents predict would have highs of at least 95° F?

____

4. A survey shows that 67% of peanut butter lovers prefer chunky-style. Out of 850 people surveyed, how many can be predicted to say they prefer chunky-style peanut butter?

____

Make a prediction based on a theoretical probability.

5. Gil rolls a number cube 78 times. How many times can he expect to roll an odd number greater than 1?

____

6. Jenna flips two pennies 105 times. How many times can she expect both coins to come up heads?

____

7. A shoebox holds same-size disks. There are 5 red, 6 white, and 7 blue disks. You pick out a disk, record its color, and return it to the box. If you repeat this process 250 times, how many times can you expect to pick either a red or white disk?

____

8. Ron draws 16 cards from a standard deck of 52. The deck is made up of equal numbers of four suits—clubs, diamonds, hearts, and spades. How many of the cards drawn can Ron expect to be spades?

____

Solve each problem.

9. During February and March, Jack is spending 7 days in the Yukon to check on endangered species. The region has snowfall that blocks roads 20 days during these months. Can Jack expect to be able to get around at least 5 of the days? Explain.

____

10. ABC Airlines has had delays on 18 of 126 recent flights. DEF Airlines has had delays 13% of the time. Which airline would you expect to provide more reliable service? Why?

____

____

Name ______________________ Date ______________ Class ______________

LESSON 11-6

Practice B

Probability of Independent and Dependent Events

Decide whether each set of events is independent or dependent. Explain your answer.

1. A student spins a spinner and chooses a Scrabble® tile

____

____

2. A boy chooses a sock from a drawer of socks, then chooses a second sock without replacing the first.

____

____

3. A student picks a raffle ticket from a box, replaces the ticket, then picks a second raffle ticket.

____

____

Find the probability of each set of independent events.

4. picking a red checker from a bag of 9 black checkers and 6 red checkers, replacing it, and picking another red checker

____

5. picking a black checker from a bag of 9 black checkers and 6 red checkers, replacing it, and picking a red checker

____

6. rolling a 1, 2, or 3 on the first roll of a 1–6 number cube and rolling a 4, 5, or 6 on the second roll of the same cube

____

Solve.

7. Randy has 4 pennies, 2 nickels, and 3 dimes in his pocket. If he randomly chooses 2 coins, what is the probability that both are dimes?

____

Name ____________________ Date __________ Class __________

LESSON 11-7

Practice B

Combinations

1. A chef has some broccoli, cauliflower, carrots, and squash to make a vegetarian dish. List the possible combinations if he uses only 3 vegetables in the dish.

____

____

____

2. Lauren, Manuel, Nick, Opal, and Pat are forming groups of two to work on a drama production. List the different combinations of students that are possible using the first initial of each name.

____

3. Keiko has seven colors of lanyard. She uses three different colors to make a key chain. How many different combinations can she choose?

____

4. On Sundays at Ice Cream Heaven, you can choose two free toppings for your sundae. The toppings are nuts, hot fudge, caramel, and sprinkles. How many different combinations of toppings can you order?

____

5. How many different three-person relay teams can be chosen from six students?

____

6. The students in Mrs. Mandel's class need to choose two class representatives from six nominated students. How many different combinations of class representatives are possible?

____

7. There are four varieties of muffins available at the Coffee Shop. How many different ways can you choose three different muffins?

____

8. How many two-person carpools are possible with seven people?

____

Name ______________________ Date ______________ Class ______________

LESSON 11-8

Practice B

Permutations

1. Joe has homework assignments for math, Spanish, and history. In how many different orders can he do his homework? ______________

2. Find the number of permutations of the letters in the word SMART. ______________

3. In how many ways can you arrange the numbers 6, 7, 8, and 9 to make a four-digit number? ______________

4. A table has 8 seats. In how many different ways can 8 people sit at the table? ______________

5. Nine mountain bikers are on a bicycle trip. In how many possible ways can they follow each other? ______________

6. Seven students are waiting in line at the cafeteria. In how many different orders can they be standing in line? ______________

7. How many permutations of the letters A through F are there? ______________

8. Ed, Martine, Sal, Carl, Paula, Terry, Ken, Leo, Ursula, and Jamie are in a race. In how many different orders can they finish? ______________

9. Find the number of permutations of the letters in the word *recognizably*. ______________

10. In how many different orders can 11 people stand in line? ______________

11. In how many different ways can a librarian arrange eight books on a shelf? ______________

12. Melinda has 15 art trophies. Write an expression that shows how many different ways she can line up her trophies on a shelf. ______________

Name ______________________ Date ______________ Class ______________

LESSON 12-1

Practice B

Solving Two-Step Equations

Solve. Check each answer.

1. $7x + 8 = 36$ ______

2. $-3y - 7 = 2$ ______

3. $4a - 13 = 19$ ______

4. $6a - 4 = -2$ ______

5. $5k + 2 = 6$ ______

6. $9m - 14 = -8$ ______

Solve.

7. $\frac{v}{4} - 3 = 5$ ______

8. $\frac{u}{5} + 3 = 1$ ______

9. $6 + \frac{z}{9} = 9$ ______

10. $-7 + \frac{f}{2} = -1$ ______

11. $9 + \frac{w}{4} = -5$ ______

12. $\frac{e}{7} - 3 = -5$ ______

13. $-8 + \frac{d}{5} = 2$ ______

14. $\frac{u}{5} + 3 = 6$ ______

15. $\frac{f}{-3} + 5 = 8$ ______

16. Two years of local Internet service costs $685, including the installation fee of $85. What is the monthly fee?

____

Name ____________________ Date ____________ Class ____________

LESSON 12-2

Practice B

Solving Multi-Step Equations

Solve.

1. $15x - 8 - 3x = 16$

2. $5n + 3 + 4n = 30$

3. $h - 6 + 7h = 42$

4. $-3g + 6 + 2g = 15$

5. $-2b + 7 - 3b = 2$

6. $5y + 1 + 3y = -15$

7. $4k - 14 + 3k = 21$

8. $9m + 10 - 14m = -5$

9. $-2d + 18 - 4d = 60$

10. $3(n + 5) + 2 = 26$

11. $4 - 2(v - 6) = -8$

12. $1.4 - 1.6(t + 6) = 4.6$

13. $2.4(m - 3) + 3.8 = -8.2$

14. $6 = 8(s - \frac{3}{4}) - 20$

15. $5(c + \frac{4}{5}) + 6 = 50$

16. Joel has twice as many CDs as Mariella has. Subtracting 7 from the number of CDs Joel has and dividing by 3 equals the number of CDs Blake has. If Blake has 25 CDs, how many CDs does Mariella have?

Name ______________________ Date ______________ Class ______________

LESSON 12-3

Practice B

Solving Equations with Variables on Both Sides

Group the terms with the variables on one side of the equal sign and simplify. Do not solve.

1. $10t = 6t + 24$

2. $-6x - 32 = 2x$

3. $j = 20 - 4j$

4. $-5d + 40 = 5d$

5. $9m - 28 = 2m$

6. $\frac{8}{9}x = 8 + \frac{4}{9}x$

Solve.

7. $8k = 6k - 26$

8. $32 - 5v = 3v + 8$

9. $-12y - 10 = -6y + 14$

10. $\frac{5}{8}a + 6 = \frac{3}{4}a$

11. $\frac{1}{4}n + 10 = \frac{2}{3}n$

12. $20 - \frac{1}{5}d = \frac{3}{10}d + 16$

13. Members of the Lake Shawnee Club pay \$40 per summer season plus \$7.50 each time they rent a boat. Nonmembers pay \$12.50 each time they rent a boat. How many times would both a member and a nonmember have to rent a boat in order to pay the same amount? ______________

Name ______________________ Date ______________ Class ______________

LESSON 12-4

Practice B

Inequalities

Write an inequality for each situation.

1. The temperature today will be at most 50 °F. ____________
2. The temperature tomorrow will be above 70 °F. ____________
3. Yesterday, there was less than 2 inches of rain. ____________
4. Last Monday, there was at least 3 inches of rain. ____________

Graph each inequality.

5. $t \le -2$ 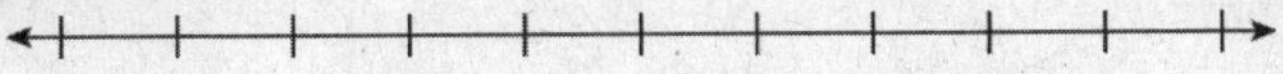

6. $j > -5$ 

7. $y \le 0$ 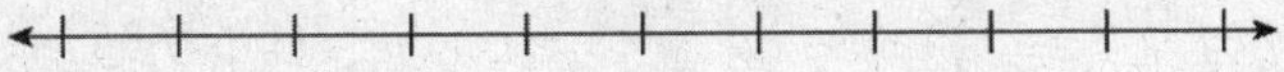

8. $b < \frac{1}{2}$ 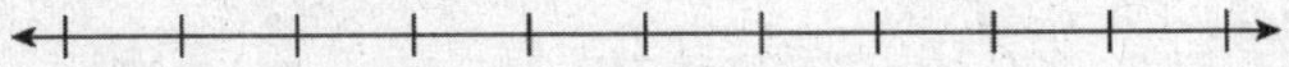

Graph each compound inequality.

9. $f > 3$ or $f < -2$ 

10. $-4 \le w \le 4$ 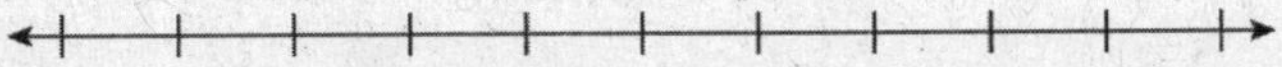

11. $b < 0$ or $b \ge 5$ 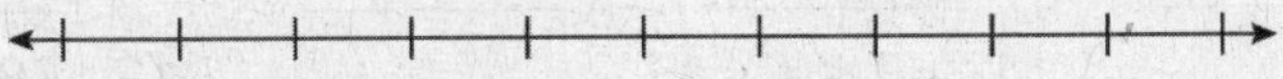

12. $y \ge 3$ or $y \le -1$ 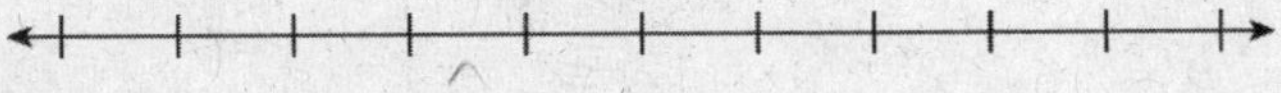

13. $-4 < m < -2$ 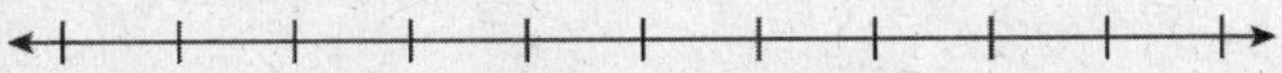

Name ______________________ Date ______________ Class ______________

LESSON 12-5

Practice B

Solving Inequalities by Adding or Subtracting

Solve. Then graph each solution set on a number line.

1. $y - 5 > -2$ ______________

2. $n + 5 \leq 11$ ______________

3. $x + 4 < -1$ ______________

4. $h + 20 > 2$ ______________

5. $p + 9 \geq -3$ ______________

6. $s - 7 < -16$ ______________

Solve. Check each answer.

7. $41 + g > 27$

8. $w + 23 \geq -18$

9. $a + 15 \leq 9$

10. $z + 27 < 16$

11. $-3 \leq t + 17$

12. $78 \geq b + 64$

13. In order for a field trip to be scheduled, at least 30 students must sign up. So far, 23 students have signed up. At least how many more students must sign up in order for the field trip to be scheduled?

____

Name ______________________ Date ______________ Class ______________

LESSON 12-6

Practice B

Solving Inequalities by Multiplying or Dividing

Solve.

1. $\frac{n}{5} \le 1.6$

2. $\frac{b}{3} > -8$

3. $\frac{a}{3} \ge -9$

4. $\frac{t}{-6} < -7$

5. $\frac{s}{-12} \le -5$

6. $\frac{r}{5.3} \le 6$

Solve. Check each answer.

7. $8c < -64$

8. $-16a \ge -24$

9. $-12t > 9$

10. $-3s \le -180$

11. $18b > -24$

12. $-6m \ge 4$

13. It cost Sophia $530 to make wind chimes. How many wind chimes must she sell at $12 apiece to make a profit?

14. It cost the Wilson children $55 to make lemonade. How many glasses must they sell at 75¢ each to make a profit?

15. Jorge's soccer team is having its annual fund raiser. The team hopes to earn at least three times as much as it did last year. Last year the team earned $87. What is the team's goal for this year?

Name ____________________ Date ______________ Class ______________

LESSON 12-7

Practice B

Solving Multi-Step Inequalities

Solve. Then graph each solution set on a number line.

1. $5x - 8 < 17$ ______________

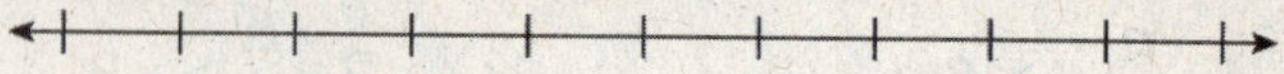

2. $3\left(\frac{r}{3} + 4\right) \geq 24$ ______________

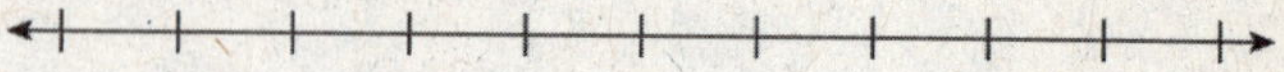

3. $3n + 7 - 7n < -5$ ______________

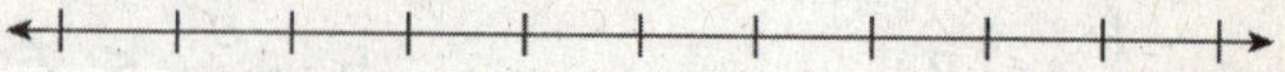

4. $\frac{z}{7} - 6 \geq -5$ ______________

5. $2(w + 36) + 10 > 32$ ______________

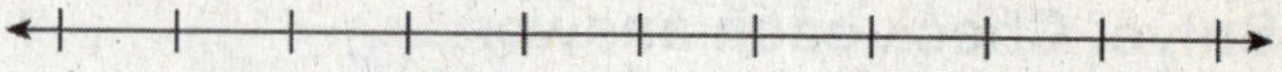

6. $\frac{u}{2} - 5 \leq -9$ ______________

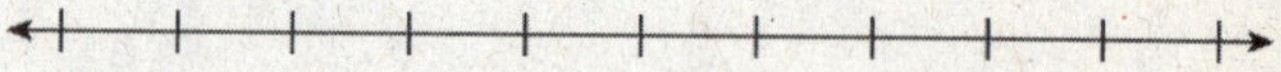

Solve.

7. $-7d + 8 > 29$

____

8. $4(g - 3) + 1 \leq 5$

____

9. $12 - 3b < 9$

____

10. $2(-a - 8) - 15 < 9$

____

11. $9 + \frac{c}{6} \leq 17$

____

12. $\frac{1}{3}p - 8 - p \geq 4$

____

13. Fifty students in the seventh grade are trying to raise at least $2,000 for sports supplies. They have already raised $750. How much should each student raise, on average, in order to meet the goal?

____